EXPLORING GENAIOPS

Empowering Leaders and Innovators To Operationalise Generative AI

Harrison Kirby

GenAIOps

CONTENTS

FOREWORD

Glen Robinson – National Technology Officer, Microsoft UK

Why is this? My 'Big Boss' Satya Nadella talks about how for years humans have had to learn to understand computers, learn their language which still remains alien to most.

But with GenAI, humans have learnt to be more human-like, understand our language so we can now interact with them as we would other humans.

The democratisation effect of this technology cannot be understated. It empowers anyone who is able to speak or write in almost any language, to now unlock the value of incredibly powerful digital systems. We've moved a long way past getting Dalli-e to create fun images and asking ChatGPT to suggest a good vegan restaurant near me. The utility of the technology as a gateway into a myriad of connected digital services will drive value that we have never experienced before so broadly across a global population.

The technology itself is still in its early stages of maturity, so we have lots more to come. GenAI and LLM's have existed conceptually since 2017 thanks to Google's research on the Transformer model architecture. We are already in a world where fine tuning, RAG, and SLM's are all improvements on the original models we created and all improve aspects of accuracy, context and speed.

But as with any new technology shift there is governance and risk to deal with and GenAI is no exception. For this it will require an operating model that spans the entire business. It will require new skills and new tools. This is the same need as any technology shift we have seen before.

That's why I'm so excited about GenAIOps. This is the solution to the evolving needs of organisations looking to maximise value from Generative AI. As a framework it is also in its infancy, and just like DevOps, MLOps, LLMOps that have come before it, it will require input from a diverse and passionate community to help capture the specifics and nuances that GenAI presents so that the framework can make sure organisations and individuals are setup for success.

That to me sounds super exciting. I hope you agree and I look forward to joining many of you on this journey –

GenAIOps

"Generative AI, or GenAI, will be the most transformative technology of our lifetime." – Glen Robinson, National technology officer, Microsoft UK.

PREFACE

The earliest known examples of written language are the Sumerian cuneiform scripts, which date back to around 3400 BCE. These ancient texts were created to store and convey information for future readers. Imagine, even our ancestors knew that writing things down was a smart move – like the world's first sticky note! This process of recording and sharing knowledge has been the backbone of human progress ever since.

Up until now, the limitations of digital technology and AI have made it challenging to fully understand and process human language, especially when it comes to interpreting large sets of unstructured data such as insurance policies, legal documents, and other extensive texts. This has meant that valuable information within PDFs, Word documents, and other formats has often been locked away, inaccessible for broader analysis and use.

Generative AI, built from human text, is intrinsically linked to, and embedded in human language mechanisms. It has the capability to understand, interpret, and generate human-like text, thereby unlocking the vast amounts of information previously trapped in unstructured formats. This marks a significant shift in knowledge and how it can be accessed and utilised.

In my view, Generative AI is poised to transform humanity more profoundly than any previous innovation, including the advent of the Cloud and the Internet. While these were significant advancements, Generative AI marks a new era in human evolution, comparable to the invention of the wheel or the perfecting of a cup of tea. However, to truly unlock its potential, and operationalise AI, we must make it work for us by evolving in three key areas;

First, we need to shift our perceptions. We must move beyond the sci-fi dystopias often portrayed by the media and understand the truth: how AI can genuinely change our lives. To do this, we must elevate our perception of ourselves and learn to approach these new tools in the right way.

Second, we need to shake up our core principles and invent new ones along the way. Clinging to outdated methods or attempting to retrofit innovation into legacy systems is never the right approach, and this is something we will tackle in this book. We must innovate, adapt and develop new strategies that leverage the unique capabilities of generative AI.

Finally, we must master the technology itself. Understanding the intricacies of generative AI is crucial to meet the expectations of our newfound perceptions. It should be truthful, fast, innovative, comprehensive, secure and cost effective – that is HARD to do, but a great challenge to tackle, nonetheless.

Lots to do then!

"Generative AI is the most powerful tool for creativity that has ever been created. It has the potential to unleash a new era of human innovation." – Elon Musk

Introduction

Generative AI represents a groundbreaking advancement in artificial intelligence, empowering machines to create content such as text, images, music, and more. Unlike traditional AI models that focus on classification or prediction, Generative AI excels at generating new data that mirrors the patterns and structures of its training data. This revolutionary capability opens a multitude of applications across various industries, from automated content creation and innovative design to advanced data augmentation and personalised customer experiences.

In essence, Generative AI is not just about making existing processes more efficient (although it can do that); it's about creating entirely new ways of working and new possibilities in entirely new ways. For instance, in the field of healthcare, generative AI will revolutionise medicine. Traditionally, creating tailored treatment plans for patients required extensive manual analysis and could take a significant amount of time. With generative AI, it's possible to analyse a patient's genetic information, medical history, and lifestyle data to generate customised treatment options in a fraction of the time. This isn't the realm of science fiction, it's the exciting reality that Generative AI brings to life.

This technology works by learning from vast amounts of data and then using that knowledge and understanding to produce original content. Imagine it as training a chef with recipes from all the world's cuisines, and then watching them invent a completely new dish that blends these influences in a unique way. The implications are vast and transformative, offering businesses and creators tools to push the boundaries of what's possible.

As we stand on the brink of this new era, the challenge lies in operationalising Generative AI effectively. It's not just about having the technology but integrating it into our workflows, organisations and culture to truly harness its potential.

GenAIOps

The possibility of Generative AI (GenAI) adoption has become widespread, thanks to the availability of pay-as-you-go APIs and the open-source community, which has made this transformative technology accessible to businesses of all sizes. However, in turn this democratisation of AI brings immense pressure on innovators globally to deliver next-generation capabilities through GenAI. It's no longer just data scientists and data engineers who need to be involved - everyone from software developers to product managers must now understand and implement GenAI solutions.

Unlike traditional application development, data engineering, and AI/ML, there is a stark lack of guidance on building and operationalising reliable and effective GenAI systems. Innovators often find themselves bewildered, struggling to grasp the fundamental concepts of how to interact with Generative AI. This situation underscores the urgent need for a comprehensive methodology that addresses both the technical and user-experience aspects of GenAI.

Enter GenAIOps, an emerging methodology designed to make the AI revolution accessible and practical for everyone.

GenAIOps (Generative AI Operations) is an evolving framework that builds upon established frameworks like DevOps, MLOps, and LLMOps. It is designed to equip teams with the adaptive culture, methodologies, and practices required to effectively address the distinctive complexities, scalability needs, and security challenges posed by generative AI throughout the development and operational lifecycle.

While it is still early to compile a fully evidence-based, definitive guide on this framework, we now have sufficient experience and resources to explore tangible methodologies, principles and practices to develop and operationalise Generative AI.

As such, in this exploration, you will find:

- ❖ **Its Harder Than We Thought** – A Look At Why Enterprise Adoption Has Not Been As Quick As Anticipated
- ❖ **The Five Levels of Complexity** – Understanding The Complexity Involved In Developing and Operationalising GenAI
- ❖ **The 6 Guiding Principles** - Guiding Your AI Journey Through All Dimensions
- ❖ **The 6 Pillars of Best Practices** – Tools and Practices to Help Develop and Operate Generative AI
- ❖ **GenAIOps Future Perspectives** - Illustrating How the Near-Term Future Will Shape Our Evolution and GenAIOps Itself

GenAIOps

Introduction

Once a new technology rolls over you, if you're not part of the steamroller, you're part of the road." – Stewart Brand

THIS IS HARDER THAN WE THOUGHT

As we dive deeper into the world of Generative AI, it's clear that the road to success is more complicated than many anticipated. While the introduction of Generative AI sparked a wave of excitement across industries, the reality is that the technology has proven more challenging to implement at the enterprise level than initially expected.

We stand at the intersection of immense opportunity and significant difficulty. As more businesses adopt Generative AI models from hyperscalers like OpenAI, Microsoft, and Google, we find ourselves grappling with the complexities of deep learning systems, the nuances of generative capabilities, and the significant gap between expectations and reality.

Despite the rapid advances in AI technology, the enterprise-level adoption of Generative AI has been slower and more challenging than expected. The inherent difficulties stem not from the lack of potential, but from the unforeseen obstacles in customising, scaling, and operationalising these systems in a way that meets the specific needs of organisations.

It's important to understand why Generative AI, despite its promise, has been harder to operationalise than we thought. Let's explore some of the key challenges.

1. Deep Learning Models: Not a Plug-and-Play Solution

At the core of Generative AI are deep learning models—neural networks with multiple layers of interconnected nodes (or "neurons"), inspired loosely by the structure of the human brain. These models form the foundation of modern Generative AI systems, enabling them to perform astonishing tasks like writing coherent paragraphs, generating images, or even coding software. But as impressive as they are, it's crucial to dispel the myth: deep learning is not magic. For all their power, deep learning models are inherently complex, opaque, and difficult to control.

To the casual observer, the idea of a machine "learning" from massive datasets and then generating new, original content may seem almost like sorcery. However, the reality is far more grounded in mathematics, statistics, and computation, and the inner workings of these models introduce several layers of complexity that enterprises must reckon with.

How Deep Learning Really Works

At its heart, deep learning relies on pattern recognition. During the training process, deep learning models analyse vast amounts of data, identifying statistical relationships between inputs (like text or images) and desired outputs (like correctly identifying an image or generating coherent text). Through countless iterations and adjustments, the model "learns" to produce outputs that approximate human-like content generation.

However, these models do not "understand" the content in the way humans do. A deep learning model generates language by predicting what word, phrase, or structure is most likely to follow a given input, based on patterns it has observed in its training data. It is not "thinking" or applying reasoning. In essence, these models are highly sophisticated systems for calculating probabilities based on historical data, not engines of creativity or insight.

This is a crucial distinction for enterprises. While a deep learning model might output what appears to be a perfectly crafted paragraph or an insightful recommendation, it is merely performing statistical analysis. There is no underlying comprehension, context awareness, or intentionality in its outputs.

The Challenge of Generalisation vs. Specialisation

One of the biggest challenges enterprises face with deep learning models is the tension between generalisation and specialisation. When pre-trained on large datasets, such as the entire corpus of publicly available internet text, these models develop broad knowledge across various domains. This broad knowledge enables generative models to answer general questions or provide generic responses effectively.

However, most enterprise applications require specialised knowledge. A generative AI system tailored for a legal firm, for example, needs to understand legal terminology, contractual nuances, and regional regulations. Similarly, a healthcare application needs to be familiar with medical diagnostics, patient confidentiality laws, and healthcare workflows.

Fine-tuning a model to perform well in a specific domain is much more difficult than it sounds. When you fine-tune a model on specialised data, there's a risk of overfitting—where the model becomes too specialised to the new data and loses its ability to generalise. This balancing act between maintaining a broad, generalisable understanding while incorporating domain-specific expertise is extraordinarily tricky. Most enterprises do not have the resources or expertise to walk this fine line successfully.

The Black Box Problem

1. Deep Learning Models: Not a Plug-and-Play Solution

Deep learning models, especially large language models, are often referred to as "black boxes." This means that while we can observe the inputs and outputs of the model, it is extremely difficult, if not impossible, to fully understand how the model arrives at a particular result.

Unlike traditional software, where every step of the process is explicitly programmed and can be traced, deep learning models make decisions based on millions (or even billions) of parameters that adjust dynamically during training. These parameters are fine-tuned during the learning process, but even the engineers who built the models often cannot pinpoint why the model produced a specific output.

This lack of transparency poses significant risks for enterprises. When a generative AI model makes an error—say, generating incorrect financial advice or misclassifying sensitive medical information—troubleshooting the model's internal decision-making is nearly impossible. Businesses are left with few options but to retrain the model or layer human oversight into every step of the AI's workflow.

Bias and Misalignment with Reality

Another inherent limitation of deep learning is that models are only as good as the data they are trained on. Since these models are trained on vast datasets, often scraped from the web, they can unintentionally pick up and amplify biases present in the data. Whether it's gender, racial, or cultural biases, deep learning models reflect the patterns they have seen, which can lead to problematic outputs when deployed in real-world scenarios.

For example, if a model is trained predominantly on data that reflects one cultural viewpoint, it may generate outputs that misrepresent or overlook other perspectives. Similarly, if trained on historical hiring data from an industry that has skewed towards particular demographics, the model might perpetuate those same biases in recruitment suggestions or evaluations.

Moreover, because these models generate outputs by "mirroring" patterns in the data, they can often produce responses that sound plausible but are completely factually incorrect. This is a significant issue for enterprises relying on generative AI for customer support, decision-making, or even regulatory compliance. The outputs may be grammatically perfect and sound authoritative, but they can be wildly inaccurate.

2. The Data Dilemma "Crap In, Crap Out"

The phrase "crap in, crap out" is a simple but powerful way to explain one of the fundamental truths of Generative AI: the quality of inputs—whether it's training data, prompts, or retrieval-augmented generation (RAG)—directly impacts the quality of outputs. No matter how advanced or powerful the AI model, if the information it receives is flawed, unstructured, biased, or irrelevant, the results will mirror those imperfections.

This concept goes beyond just the initial training phase of a model. Every interaction with Generative AI, whether it's providing a prompt or using external data sources to assist in retrieval-augmented generation (RAG), follows the same principle. For instance, a well-constructed prompt can lead to accurate, relevant outputs, while a poorly phrased prompt might result in vague, incorrect, or misleading responses. Similarly, using unreliable or incomplete external data to augment a model's responses only amplifies errors and misinformation.

For enterprises, this "crap in, crap out" dynamic is especially problematic. When businesses rely on AI models for critical tasks—like generating customer-facing content, decision support, or automating workflows—errors in inputs can cause major issues downstream. A model responding to customer inquiries with incomplete or inaccurate data, for example, risks damaging brand reputation and customer trust. Similarly, an AI tasked with generating legal contracts or financial advice, if fed inconsistent or outdated information, can lead to costly mistakes.

Moreover, the problem doesn't stop with training data. As AI systems grow more integrated into business operations, they depend on continuous interaction—with employees feeding the models new prompts, customers interacting via chatbots, or external data being fed in real-time for applications like dynamic product recommendations. If these inputs are of poor quality, even the most finely-tuned models will fail to perform as expected. In the case of retrieval-augmented generation (RAG), where models pull external sources to enhance their outputs, the system is only as good as the reliability and relevance of those sources.

Additionally, the input complexity only grows as enterprises scale. When multiple departments provide different types of data or use Generative AI across varied use cases (from marketing to operations), maintaining high-quality inputs becomes increasingly difficult. Siloed data, inconsistent input standards, or unstructured queries can further degrade the performance of AI, leading to suboptimal outputs across the organisation.

Ultimately, no matter how advanced a Generative AI model is, its success relies on the quality of every input it receives. From data used for training to prompts and external information sources used during operation, the "crap in, crap out" principle underscores the importance of maintaining high-quality data, precise queries, and reliable information sources in all AI interactions. Without these, even the best technology will fall short of delivering meaningful, accurate, and effective results.

3. Cost and Infrastructure Challenges

One of the most significant, yet often underestimated, challenges with Generative AI adoption is the cost structure tied to pay-as-you-go (PAYG) models and token-based pricing offered by hyperscalers like OpenAI, Google, and Microsoft. While these pricing models provide flexibility, allowing enterprises to pay only for what they use, they can quickly become a financial burden as usage scales—especially in production environments where generative models are integrated into critical operations.

At the heart of most Generative AI APIs is the concept of tokens—units that represent chunks of data, such as words, characters, or even fragments of language models' operations. Every time an enterprise interacts with a model to generate content—whether it's a piece of text, a chatbot response, or an image—tokens are consumed. The cost per API call depends on the number of tokens processed, meaning that longer or more complex outputs can significantly increase costs. This presents an ongoing dilemma for businesses: the more sophisticated or detailed the AI output, the more expensive it becomes.

In practical terms, while PAYG models seem attractive for small-scale use, costs can spiral out of control in large-scale deployments. For example, a business using Generative AI to automate customer service across thousands of daily interactions will quickly accumulate high token usage, resulting in mounting expenses. Each response generated by the AI consumes tokens, and even a modest increase in interaction complexity (such as longer answers or more detailed customer queries) can lead to exponential cost growth. These costs are not always predictable, making it difficult for businesses to manage their AI budgets effectively.

Moreover, real-time applications—such as chatbots,

recommendation engines, or personalised marketing systems—require frequent API calls, further driving up token consumption and costs. These operational expenses are often much higher than anticipated during initial experimentation phases, where usage is typically low and controlled. When moving from pilot projects to full-scale deployments, many businesses face the harsh reality of unsustainable costs, leading them to either scale back their ambitions or seek alternative, cost-saving measures.

Additionally, enterprises relying heavily on hyperscaler APIs run into the challenge of cost spikes during peak usage periods. For instance, seasonal demand surges or marketing campaigns that drive up customer engagement can lead to a sharp increase in API calls, and therefore token usage, causing unexpected jumps in cloud bills. This unpredictability in cost structure makes it difficult for companies to plan long-term budgets or justify ROI, especially when AI-driven processes become a core part of the business.

Lastly, as businesses become more reliant on hyperscaler APIs, they face vendor lock-in, which exacerbates the cost issue. Transitioning away from one provider to another, or developing in-house AI capabilities, is complex and costly, further limiting a company's ability to optimise infrastructure or reduce costs.

In summary, while PAYG and token-based pricing models provide an accessible entry point for Generative AI experimentation, they can become major cost drivers at scale. For enterprises aiming to integrate AI deeply into their operations, these pricing models often introduce hidden costs and long-term financial constraints, leading them to reconsider the true economic feasibility of large-scale AI adoption.

4. Ethical and Reputational Risks

Generative AI models are not inherently ethical or free from bias. Since these models are trained on vast datasets drawn from publicly available sources such as the internet, social media, and digital repositories, they inevitably inherit the biases, inaccuracies, and imperfections present in those data sets. As a result, generative AI can produce content that unintentionally reflects racial, gender, or cultural biases, or worse, generates offensive or inappropriate outputs. This poses a significant reputational risk for enterprises, especially when these models are used in customer-facing applications, such as marketing content creation, virtual assistants, or chatbots.

The unpredictability of these models means that even with proper training, they can occasionally generate factually incorrect or misleading information, which can erode customer trust and damage brand reputation. For enterprises operating in industries where accuracy and neutrality are paramount—such as legal services, healthcare, or financial advisory—these missteps could have far-reaching consequences, leading to legal liability, customer attrition, and public relations crises.

To mitigate these risks, many organisations are being forced to implement additional layers of governance and human oversight. These governance structures involve continuously evaluating AI outputs, implementing ethical guidelines, and ensuring compliance with industry-specific regulations. However, introducing these measures not only increases operational complexity but also slows down the deployment and scaling of AI systems, as every output may require review by legal, compliance, or domain experts before release. In regulated industries like healthcare and finance, the compliance burden is even more significant, as enterprises must ensure that AI-generated outputs comply with GDPR, HIPAA, and other stringent data privacy and security regulations. This often requires manual intervention, which reduces the efficiency that AI adoption originally promised.

In short, while Generative AI can provide transformative benefits, its ethical and reputational risks require organisations to invest heavily in governance frameworks, risk management, and human oversight, adding complexity to AI operations that many companies did not foresee.

5. The Skills Gap

While tools for Generative AI are becoming increasingly accessible, the skills gap in operating these tools effectively remains a major hurdle for enterprises. Unlike traditional software systems, Generative AI requires specialised knowledge across multiple domains, including data science, machine learning, deep learning architecture, and natural language processing (NLP). This diversity in required expertise means that most businesses lack the in-house talent necessary to fully design, implement, and manage generative AI systems at scale.

One of the key issues is that Generative AI systems are not intuitive for non-technical teams. Even with user-friendly interfaces provided by hyperscalers, the underlying complexities—such as fine-tuning models, managing token consumption, addressing biases, and ensuring relevance of outputs—require a deep technical understanding. Most enterprises struggle with interpreting AI outputs and aligning them with business objectives, especially in industries where subject-matter expertise is essential to understanding the nuances of generated content.

Additionally, many decision-makers lack awareness of AI limitations and potential risks, leading to over-reliance on these models without fully understanding their weaknesses. This often results in suboptimal AI deployments that fail to meet business goals or worse, damage the organisation's reputation. Bridging this gap requires not just hiring more technical talent, but also upskilling non-technical staff to understand how Generative AI fits into broader business strategies.

Enterprises are realising that AI literacy needs to extend beyond data scientists and engineers. Executives, project managers, and domain experts need to be trained to ask the right questions, understand AI limitations, and implement effective oversight. Unfortunately, this shift in organisational mindset is a slow process, and until the majority of staff can work effectively with Generative AI, enterprises will struggle to fully leverage its potential.

Conclusion

Generative AI, while incredibly powerful, presents a host of challenges that many enterprises are only beginning to grasp. Deep learning models, though sophisticated, are not magic solutions; they require extensive customisation and come with significant complexity, including the balance between generalisation and specialisation. The "black box" nature of these systems makes it difficult to understand or control their outputs, while the vast amounts of data needed for fine-tuning only compound the problem. Enterprises also face high costs, both in terms of infrastructure and ongoing operation, and must navigate ethical and reputational risks as these models can generate biased or incorrect content. Finally, the lack of internal expertise means that most organisations are not yet equipped to fully leverage the technology. These obstacles illustrate why operationalising Generative AI is far harder than anticipated, demanding careful strategy, expertise, and resources to unlock its true potential.

5. The Skills Gap

Only variety (in the regulator) can destroy variety (in the system being regulated) – Ashby's Law

So now you know! There's a mountain to climb, and before climbing Everest it's usually a good idea to tackle your local hill.....

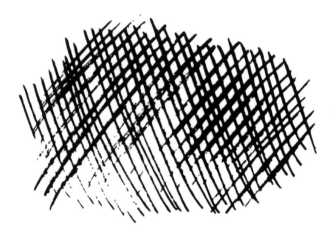

THE FIVE LEVELS OF COMPLEXITY

As we embark on our journey to explore GenAIOps, it's crucial to understand that Generative AI isn't a monolithic technology but a multifaceted one with varying degrees of complexity. These complexities influence how we develop, implement, and interact with AI systems. By dissecting Generative AI into five distinct levels of complexity, we can better appreciate the challenges and opportunities at each stage.

This chapter aims to illuminate these five levels, providing clarity on what each entail and how they build upon one another. By the end, you'll have a deeper understanding of the intricacies involved in

Generative AI's capabilities can be categorised into five progressive levels, each representing an increase in complexity, functionality, and integration. These levels are:

THE FIVE LEVELS OF COMPLEXITY

1. Level 1: Basic Content Generation

2. Level 2: Context-Aware Generation

3. Level 3: Data-Driven Generation Using Large External Corpora

4. Level 4: Integrated System Interaction

5. Level 5: Autonomous End-to-End Process Automation

Let's delve into each level to uncover the complexities involved.

Level 1: Basic Content Generation

Definition

At this foundational level, Generative AI performs simple, standalone tasks based solely on immediate text input. It operates without contextual awareness or integration with external data sources or systems.

Key Characteristics

- ❖ Immediate Input Processing - The AI responds directly to the input provided, without considering any additional context.

- ❖ No Memory or Contextual Awareness - It lacks the ability to remember previous interactions or understand the broader context.

- ❖ Isolated Functionality - Functions independently, not connected to other systems or databases.

- ❖ Limited Complexity - Handles straightforward tasks that don't require advanced understanding or reasoning.

Examples

- ❖ Text Summarisation - Summarising a single article without referencing external information.

- ❖ Basic Translation - Translating a paragraph without considering the context of previous sentences.

- ❖ Simple Email Drafting - Generating a basic email reply from a short prompt.

- ❖ Keyword Extraction: Identifying key terms from a text snippet.

Appreciating the Complexity

While seemingly simple, achieving effective basic content generation requires a well-trained language model capable of understanding and producing human language. Challenges at this level include ensuring grammatical correctness and relevance to the input prompt. It serves as the building block for more complex applications.

Level 2: Context-Aware Generation

Definition

This level introduces the ability to incorporate immediate text context or short-term memory within a single interaction. The AI produces more relevant and coherent outputs by considering the context of the current session but doesn't utilise extensive external data or integrate with other systems.

Key Characteristics

* Session-Based Memory - Remembers information within the current interaction.

* Contextual Responses - Generates outputs influenced by prior inputs in the session.

* No External Data Integration - Doesn't access large external datasets beyond the session context.

* Enhanced Personalisation - Provides more tailored responses based on immediate context.

Examples

* Conversational AI - Maintaining context in a text-based chat, allowing for coherent and relevant responses.

* Contextual Email Responses - Crafting email replies that consider the entire email thread for continuity.

* Adaptive Learning Content - Adjusting educational materials based on the learner's recent interactions.

* Personalised Recommendations - Suggesting articles based on the user's reading history within a session.

Appreciating the Complexity

At this level, the AI must handle context management, which involves retaining and appropriately utilising information from earlier in the interaction. This adds complexity as the AI needs to maintain coherence and relevance over multiple exchanges, enhancing user experience but requiring more sophisticated processing.

Level 3: Data-Driven Generation Using Large External Corpora

Definition

Generative AI leverages extensive external text datasets to enhance its outputs. It accesses and utilises large-scale data within a single domain or system without integrating multiple external systems.

Key Characteristics

- ❖ Utilisation of Large Text Datasets - Accesses vast amounts of data to generate informed responses.

- ❖ Domain-Specific Expertise - Operates within a specific domain (e.g., legal, medical, academic).

- ❖ No System Integration - Functions without connecting to other external systems.

- ❖ Informed and Accurate Responses - Provides outputs reflecting deep knowledge from extensive data.

Examples

- ❖ Research Summarisation - Analysing numerous academic papers to generate comprehensive literature reviews.

- ❖ Historical Document Analysis - Extracting insights from large collections of historical texts.

- ❖ Advanced Q&A Systems - Providing detailed answers to complex questions using extensive text databases.

- ❖ Legal Document Analysis - Summarising and interpreting legal texts from vast corpora.

Appreciating the Complexity

The AI now handles vast amounts of unstructured text data,

requiring advanced capabilities in data processing and understanding. Challenges include managing data quality, ensuring relevance, and preventing information overload. The AI must also handle nuances and terminologies specific to the domain.

Level 4: Integrated System Interaction

Definition

At this level, Generative AI interacts with multiple external systems or platforms, integrating text data and functionalities to perform complex tasks. It operates under predefined parameters without autonomous decision-making beyond its programming.

Key Characteristics

- ❖ System Integration - Connects with multiple platforms (e.g., databases, APIs).

- ❖ Coordinated Functionality - Works with different systems to accomplish tasks.

- ❖ Operates Under Predefined Parameters - Functions within set guidelines and rules.

- ❖ Enhanced Capabilities Through Integration - Leverages external systems for advanced functionalities.

Examples

- ❖ Intelligent Document Processing - Extracting information from unstructured text documents and updating enterprise databases.

- ❖ Automated Customer Support - Accessing CRM systems to provide personalised text responses.

- ❖ Content Moderation - Analysing and filtering user-generated text content across platforms.

- ❖ Multilingual Communication - Translating and routing text communications in different languages.

Appreciating the Complexity

Integration introduces significant complexity. The AI must communicate with various systems, each with its own protocols and data formats. Ensuring seamless interaction requires robust integration strategies. Additionally, maintaining data security and privacy across systems becomes critical.

Level 5: Autonomous End-to-End Process Automation

Definition

This advanced level involves the AI autonomously managing entire text-based processes across multiple integrated systems. It makes independent decisions and adapts without human intervention, effectively automating complex workflows.

Key Characteristics

❖ Autonomous Operation - Functions without human oversight.

❖ End-to-End Process Management - Handles all stages of a process from initiation to completion.

❖ Dynamic Adaptation - Adjusts operations in response to new data or changes.

❖ Multi-System Coordination - Seamlessly integrates and coordinates across systems.

❖ Complex Decision-Making Abilities - Makes informed decisions based on real-time data.

Examples

❖ Automated Content Generation and Distribution - AI writes and distributes articles based on real-time analysis.

❖ Legal Document Review Automation - End-to-end processing of legal documents, including analysis and updates.

❖ Personalised News Delivery - Curating and delivering news articles tailored to individual preferences.

❖ Educational Content Curation and Distribution - Creating and distributing personalised educational materials.

Appreciating the Complexity

At this pinnacle of complexity, the AI must not only integrate with multiple systems but also operate autonomously. It needs advanced decision-making capabilities, adapting to new information and circumstances. Challenges include ensuring reliability, managing exceptions, and upholding ethical standards without human intervention.

Conclusion

To successfully navigate the complexities of Generative AI from Level 1 to Level 5, a human-centric, principle-led approach supported by best practices is essential. As AI systems grow in complexity and autonomy, keeping human needs and values at the forefront ensures that technology serves to enhance user experiences and societal benefits.

Note to the Reader

As you reflect on the content of this chapter, consider where your organisation or projects currently sit within these levels. What challenges have you encountered, and how might understanding these complexities inform your approach moving forward?

Level 5: Autonomous End-to-End Process Automation

"AI will be part of every industry, enhancing our abilities in ways we can't even imagine yet." – Jeff Bezos

Congratulations! Hopefully you have realised or reaffirmed your position on the challenges afoot, let's get onto solutions. It's still early doors, and we have a long way to go to define this as "standards", but the 6 guiding principles and 6 pillars of best practices in the following chapter will help you overcome the challenges – if not, sorry this book is non refundable ;)

The 6 Guiding Principles

The principles of GenAIOps are designed to guide your thought process and decision-making at every stage of developing, deploying, and managing generative AI systems. By adhering to these principles, you verify that your AI initiatives are not only effective and reliable but also aligned with your organisation's goals and values. Let's explore these principles in detail:

Agentic-Based Development

The Agentic-Based Development principle promotes a modular approach to designing generative AI systems by breaking them down into specialised, autonomous agents rather than a single, integrated system. This method enhances flexibility, scalability, and maintainability, allowing organisations to modify or scale individual components independently and improve overall system resilience. The principle advocates for defining agents based on their specific

50

tasks and ensuring they can operate autonomously while interacting seamlessly with other agents.

Embody DevOps

The Embody DevOps principle integrates DevOps methodologies into the development and management of AI systems. It emphasises continuous integration (CI), continuous delivery (CD), and continuous feedback to ensure efficient, reliable and scalable AI development. By promoting seamless workflows, iterative experimentation, and ongoing feedback, this principle aims to enhance the overall operational excellence of AI systems and foster a collaborative culture between development and operations teams.

Progressive Integration

The Progressive Integration principle advocates for a gradual approach to deploying AI systems, emphasising the importance of building trust over time. By implementing AI solutions incrementally, organisations can demonstrate reliability and effectiveness, reduce risks, and adapt based on feedback. This phased approach allows for smoother adoption, enhanced user confidence, and cost-effective investments, ensuring AI systems meet user needs and align with organisational goals.

Driven by Evaluation

Driven by Evaluation stresses the need for continuous assessment and measurement of AI systems' performance. Traditional evaluation methods may fall short for generative AI, so this principle advocates for dynamic, context-sensitive evaluation mechanisms. By incorporating tailored metrics, user feedback, and iterative refinement, organisations can maintain high standards of quality, relevance, and user satisfaction, ensuring ongoing improvement and transparency in AI performance.

Keep it Simple

The Keep It Simple principle emphasises simplicity in AI design and implementation. By focusing on clear, practical solutions and avoiding unnecessary complexity, this approach aims to make AI systems easier to understand, manage, and maintain. Simplicity reduces the risk of errors, enhances efficiency, and improves scalability, contributing to more robust and cost-effective AI solutions. Adopting this principle involves clear requirements, modular design, and iterative development.

Focus on Value

The Focus on Value principle highlights the importance of delivering tangible value through AI initiatives. It ensures that AI systems are aligned with organisational goals, address real user needs, and drive business improvements. By defining clear value objectives, adopting value-driven frameworks, and continuously validating impact, organisations can maximise ROI, enhance user satisfaction, and support sustainable AI success. This principle promotes a value-centric approach to AI development and implementation. Embrace these principles, and you will be ready to create and manage generative AI systems that are both innovative and impactful. As Generative AI continues to evolve, sticking to these guiding principles will keep you at the cutting edge of technology, driving success for your organisation and delivering exceptional value to your stakeholders.

Agentic-Based Development

Role of the Principle

The Agentic-Based Development principle emphasises designing generative AI systems using an agentic-based approach, akin to microservices in software development. Instead of creating a single, monolithic AI system, this principle advocates for the development of specialised agents, each focused on a specific task or area. This modular approach is crucial for enhancing the flexibility, scalability, and maintainability of AI systems.

Holistic Benefits

- ❖ Flexibility - By dividing the AI system into smaller, task-specific agents, you can easily modify, upgrade, or replace individual components without disrupting the entire system.
- ❖ Scalability - Specialised agents can be scaled independently based on the demand and complexity of their respective tasks, ensuring efficient resource utilisation.
- ❖ Maintainability - Modular systems are easier to troubleshoot and maintain. Issues can be isolated and addressed within individual agents without affecting the broader system.
- ❖ Resilience - Failure in one agent does not necessarily impact the entire system, increasing the overall resilience and reliability of the AI deployment.
- ❖ Collaboration - Different teams can work on separate agents simultaneously, promoting parallel development and faster iterations.

How to Define an Agent

An agent in the context of Generative AI is a specialised, autonomous unit designed to perform a specific function or task within the broader AI system. Here are the key characteristics of an agent:

- ❖ Specialisation - Each agent focuses on a specific area of functionality, such as data processing, natural language understanding, or image generation.
- ❖ Autonomy - Agents operate independently and can make decisions or perform tasks without needing constant external guidance.
- ❖ Interoperability - Agents communicate and interact with other agents and systems through well-defined interfaces and protocols.
- ❖ Reusability - Agents are designed to be reusable across different projects and applications, promoting consistency and efficiency.

How to Apply the Principle

- ❖ Identify Tasks - Break down the overall functionality of your AI system into discrete tasks that can be handled by individual agents. This involves a thorough analysis of the AI's objectives, and the processes needed to achieve them.
- ❖ Design Agents - Define the scope, responsibilities, and interfaces of each agent. Verify that each agent has a clear, focused role and that it can operate independently while interacting seamlessly with other agents.
- ❖ Develop Modular Components - Implement each agent as a separate, modular component. Use microservices architecture principles to ensure each agent is loosely coupled and can be developed, deployed, and scaled independently.
- ❖ Ensure Interoperability - Establish robust communication protocols and APIs to facilitate seamless interaction between agents. This ensures that agents can work together harmoniously to achieve the system's overall goals.

❖ Iterate and Optimise - Continuously monitor the performance of individual agents and the system as a whole. Make iterative improvements to enhance functionality, efficiency, and integration.

Adopting an agentic-based approach in Generative AI development fosters a modular, scalable, and maintainable architecture. By breaking down AI systems into specialised agents, you can enhance flexibility, improve resilience, and accelerate innovation. This principle not only streamlines development processes but also ensures that AI solutions are robust, adaptable, and aligned with evolving business needs.

Embody DevOps

Role of the Principle

The Embody DevOps principle integrates DevOps methodologies into the development, deployment, and management of generative AI systems. By applying DevOps principles such as continuous integration (CI), continuous delivery (CD), and continuous feedback, this approach emphasises the importance of seamless flow, iterative experimentation, and ongoing feedback. This ensures that AI systems are developed and deployed efficiently, reliably, and consistently.

Holistic Benefits

❖ Efficiency - Streamlining the development and deployment processes reduces bottlenecks and accelerates time-to-market for AI solutions.
❖ Reliability - Continuous testing and integration verify that AI systems are robust and less prone to errors, enhancing overall reliability.
❖ Scalability - DevOps practices enable scalable development and deployment, allowing organisations to handle increasing workloads and complexity effectively.
❖ Collaboration - Promotes a culture of collaboration between development and operations teams, leading to better communication, faster problem-solving, and more innovative solutions.
❖ Flexibility - Continuous feedback and iterative improvements allow for rapid adaptation to changing requirements and new insights, ensuring that AI systems remain relevant and effective.

DevOps Concepts

The 6 Guiding Principles

❖ Continuous Integration (CI) - The practice of frequently merging code changes into a central repository where automated builds and tests are run. This ensures that the AI system is always in a releasable state.

❖ Continuous Delivery (CD) - Extends CI by automatically deploying code changes to a staging or production environment after passing all tests. This ensures that new features and fixes can be delivered quickly and safely.

❖ Continuous Feedback - Involves collecting and integrating feedback from users and stakeholders continuously to improve the AI system. This feedback loop is crucial for iterative development and enhancement.

❖ Flow - Ensures a smooth and efficient flow of work from development through to deployment, minimising delays and maximising productivity.

❖ Experimentation - Encourages a culture of experimentation where new ideas can be tested quickly and iteratively. This fosters innovation and helps in identifying the most effective solutions.

How to Apply the Principle

❖ Adopt CI/CD Pipelines - Implement continuous integration and delivery pipelines to automate the building, testing, and deployment of AI systems. Use tools like Jenkins, GitLab CI, or CircleCI to facilitate these processes.

❖ Automated Testing - Develop comprehensive automated test suites to verify that all code changes are thoroughly tested before deployment. This includes unit tests, integration tests, and end-to-end tests.

❖ Infrastructure as Code (IaC) - Use IaC tools like Terraform or AWS CloudFormation to manage and provision infrastructure. This ensures consistency and repeatability in deployment environments.

❖ Monitoring and Logging - Implement robust monitoring and logging practices to track the performance and health of AI systems. Use tools like Prometheus, Grafana, or ELK Stack to gain insights and detect issues early.

❖ Feedback Loops - Establish continuous feedback mechanisms to gather user and stakeholder input. Use this feedback to drive iterative improvements and verify that the AI system meets evolving needs.

❖ Collaborative Culture - Foster a DevOps culture that encourages collaboration between development, operations, and other stakeholders. Conduct regular retrospectives and planning sessions to align goals and improve processes.

❖ Experimentation Frameworks - Create frameworks for safe experimentation where new features and ideas can be tested in controlled environments. Use techniques like A/B testing to validate hypotheses and measure impact.

Embodying DevOps principles in the development and deployment of generative AI systems ensures efficiency, reliability, and continuous improvement. By integrating CI/CD, continuous feedback, and a culture of collaboration and experimentation, you can build robust and adaptable AI solutions. This approach not only enhances the operational excellence of AI systems but also drives innovation and responsiveness to changing business needs and user expectations.

Progressive Integration

Role of the Principle

The Progressive Integration principle highlights the importance of earning trust in generative AI systems gradually. Trust is not given instantly but built over time through consistent performance and reliability. By implementing AI solutions incrementally, you can demonstrate their effectiveness and reliability, allowing users to gain confidence in AI capabilities. This phased approach mitigates risks and facilitates smoother adoption.

Holistic Benefits

❖ Risk Mitigation - Incremental implementation helps identify and address potential issues early, reducing the risk of large-scale failures.

❖ Improved Reliability - Gradual integration allows for thorough testing and validation at each stage, ensuring that the AI system is reliable and performs as expected.

❖ Enhanced User Confidence - Building trust gradually helps users become more comfortable and confident in the AI system's capabilities.

❖ Flexibility and Adaptation - This approach provides the flexibility to adapt and refine AI systems based on feedback and performance, ensuring they meet evolving needs.

❖ Cost Efficiency - Progressive integration allows for controlled investment, reducing the financial risk associated with large-scale AI deployments.

A Note on Trust and Humans

Trust is a critical factor in the adoption of generative AI. Humans naturally tend to be cautious about new technologies, especially those that can significantly impact their work and lives. Earning trust requires demonstrating the AI system's reliability, accuracy, and alignment with human values and expectations. Transparent communication about AI capabilities and limitations, along with consistent and predictable performance, helps build this trust. Moreover, involving users in the incremental deployment process ensures they feel a sense of ownership and confidence in the AI system.

How to Apply the Principle

- ❖ Start Small - Begin with small, manageable projects or components of the AI system. Select use cases that have clear benefits and lower risks to demonstrate value quickly.
- ❖ Pilot Programs - Implement pilot programs to test AI solutions in real-world conditions. Use these pilots to gather data, assess performance, and identify any issues.
- ❖ Iterative Improvement - Based on the feedback and data from pilot programs, make iterative improvements to the AI system. Verify that each iteration addresses identified issues and enhances performance.
- ❖ Phased Rollout - Roll out the AI system in phases, gradually expanding its scope and functionality. This allows for continuous testing and validation while scaling up.
- ❖ Transparency and Communication - Maintain open and transparent communication with stakeholders throughout the integration process. Clearly explain the goals, benefits, and limitations of the AI system.
- ❖ Stakeholder Involvement - Involve key stakeholders, including end-users, in the integration process. Solicit their feedback and address their concerns to build trust and acceptance.
- ❖ Monitoring and Evaluation - Continuously monitor the AI

system's performance and evaluate its impact. Use this data to inform further improvements and ensure the system remains reliable and effective.

❖ Documentation and Training - Provide comprehensive documentation and training to users, helping them understand how to interact with the AI system and what to expect from it.

Progressive Integration is essential for building trust and confidence in generative AI systems. By adopting a phased approach, organisations can mitigate risks, enhance reliability, and verify that AI solutions are effectively meeting user needs. This principle not only fosters smoother adoption but also ensures that AI systems are continuously refined and aligned with organisational goals and user expectations. Transparent communication and stakeholder involvement are key to earning and maintaining trust in AI capabilities over time.

Driven by Evaluation

Role of the Principle

The Driven by Evaluation principle underscores the importance of continuously assessing and measuring the performance of generative AI systems. Given the subjective nature of AI outputs, traditional evaluation methods often fall short. This principle advocates for the use of new evaluation mechanisms and metrics that are tailored to the unique characteristics of generative AI. By focusing on evaluation-driven development, organisations can verify that their AI systems meet high standards of quality, relevance, and user satisfaction.

Holistic Benefits

* ❖ Quality Assurance - Continuous evaluation helps maintain high quality in AI outputs by identifying and addressing issues promptly.
* ❖ Relevance - Tailored evaluation mechanisms verify that AI systems produce outputs that are relevant and valuable to users.
* ❖ User Satisfaction - Regularly assessing AI performance from a user perspective enhances user satisfaction by aligning outputs with user needs and expectations.
* ❖ Continuous Improvement - Evaluation-driven development promotes ongoing refinement and optimisation of AI systems, ensuring they evolve and improve over time.
* ❖ Transparency and Accountability - Systematic evaluation provides a transparent and accountable framework for AI performance, building trust among stakeholders.

New Way of Thinking

Evaluating generative AI requires a shift from traditional evaluation metrics to more dynamic and context-sensitive approaches. This new way of thinking involves:

- ❖ Contextual Metrics - Developing metrics that consider the context and use case of the AI system, rather than relying solely on generic performance indicators.
- ❖ User-Centric Evaluation - Focusing on how users perceive and interact with AI outputs, incorporating user feedback and satisfaction into evaluation criteria.
- ❖ Iterative Feedback Loops - Establishing continuous feedback loops where evaluation results directly inform development cycles, promoting iterative improvements.
- ❖ Holistic Assessment - Combining quantitative metrics (e.g., accuracy, precision) with qualitative assessments (e.g., user feedback, expert reviews) to form a comprehensive evaluation strategy.

How to Apply the Principle

- ❖ Define Success Criteria - Establish clear, context-specific criteria for evaluating AI performance. These criteria should align with the goals and expectations of users and stakeholders.
- ❖ Evaluation Driven Development (EDD) - Incorporate evaluation into the development process from the outset. This approach, featured in the Usability and User-Centricity pillar, ensures that evaluation is an integral part of AI system design and iteration.
- ❖ Develop Custom Metrics - Create metrics that reflect the unique characteristics and goals of the AI system. This might include user satisfaction scores, contextual relevance measures, and performance indicators tailored to specific tasks.

- ❖ Continuous Monitoring - Implement tools and processes for continuous monitoring of AI performance. Use real-time data to assess how well the system is meeting defined criteria.
- ❖ User Feedback Integration - Actively gather and integrate user feedback into the evaluation process. This feedback should be used to refine metrics and inform system improvements.
- ❖ Iterative Testing and Refinement - Conduct regular testing cycles were evaluation results guide development efforts. Use these cycles to iteratively improve AI performance and address any issues.
- ❖ Transparent Reporting - Maintain transparent reporting practices, sharing evaluation results with stakeholders. These builds trust and demonstrates accountability in AI system performance.
- ❖ Expert Reviews - Incorporate expert reviews into the evaluation process to gain insights and validation from experienced professionals. This helps verify that the AI system meets high standards of quality and relevance.

Driving AI development by evaluation ensures that generative AI systems are continuously assessed and improved to meet high standards of quality and relevance. By adopting evaluation-driven development, organisations can align AI outputs with user needs and expectations, fostering greater satisfaction and trust. This principle encourages a shift to context-sensitive, user-centric evaluation methods, promoting ongoing refinement and optimisation of AI systems. Through systematic and transparent evaluation, organisations can build reliable, effective, and user-friendly AI solutions.

Keep it Simple

Role of the Principle

The Keep It Simple principle emphasises the importance of simplicity in the design and implementation of AI systems. By avoiding unnecessary complexity and focusing on practical, efficient solutions, this principle ensures that AI systems are easier to understand, manage, and maintain. Simplicity reduces the risk of errors and inefficiencies, making AI systems more robust and reliable.

Holistic Benefits

- ❖ Ease of Understanding - Simple designs are easier for developers and stakeholders to understand, facilitating better communication and collaboration.
- ❖ Manageability - Simpler systems are easier to manage, reducing the burden on operational and maintenance teams.
- ❖ Reduced Error Risk - Avoiding complexity minimises the potential for errors and bugs, leading to more reliable AI systems.
- ❖ Efficiency - Streamlined designs are often more efficient in terms of performance and resource utilisation.
- ❖ Scalability - Simple systems are easier to scale, as they can be extended or modified without significant reengineering.
- ❖ Cost-Effectiveness - Simplicity often leads to cost savings in development, deployment, and maintenance phases.

How to Apply the Principle

- ❖ Adopt KISS (Keep It Simple, Stupid) Principles - Embrace the traditional KISS approach, which advocates for simplicity and avoiding unnecessary complexity. Design AI systems with the simplest possible solutions that meet the requirements.
- ❖ Clear Requirements - Define clear and concise requirements

for the AI system. Focus on essential features and functionalities, avoiding the temptation to add unnecessary bells and whistles.

❖ Modular Design - Break down the AI system into smaller, modular components and utilise Agents. This allows each module to be simple and focused on a specific task, making the overall system easier to manage and understand.

❖ Iterative Development - Develop the AI system iteratively, starting with a minimal viable product (MVP) that covers the core functionalities. Gradually add features based on user feedback and performance evaluations.

❖ User-Centric Approach - Design with the end-user in mind. Verify that the AI system's interface and interactions are intuitive and straightforward, enhancing user experience and reducing the need for extensive training.

❖ Automation and Tools - Utilise automation tools and frameworks that simplify development and deployment processes. Automating repetitive tasks can reduce complexity and improve efficiency.

❖ Documentation - Maintain clear and concise documentation for the AI system. Good documentation helps developers and users understand the system's design and functionality, facilitating easier maintenance and troubleshooting.

❖ Regular Reviews - Conduct regular design and code reviews to identify and eliminate unnecessary complexity. Encourage a culture of simplicity and practicality within the development team.

❖ Feedback Loops - Establish feedback loops with users and stakeholders to gather insights on system usability and performance. Use this feedback to simplify and refine the AI system continually.

Keeping AI systems simple is crucial for their success and longevity.

By striving for simplicity in design and implementation, organisations can create AI solutions that are easy to understand, manage, and maintain. This principle aligns with the traditional KISS approach, promoting efficiency, reliability, and user satisfaction. Adopting a user-centric, modular, and iterative development process ensures that AI systems remain practical and effective, reducing the risk of errors and inefficiencies. Simplicity is not just a design choice but a strategic approach that drives better outcomes and sustainable AI solutions.

Focus on Value

Role of the Principle

The Focus on Value principle underscores the importance of prioritising the delivery of tangible value through AI initiatives. This principle ensures that AI systems are designed and implemented to address real user needs, improve business processes, and drive organisational goals. By continuously evaluating the impact of AI systems and refining them, organisations can maximise their value contribution, aligning AI efforts with strategic objectives.

Holistic Benefits

- ❖ Alignment with Business Goals - Ensuring AI initiatives are directly linked to organisational goals promotes strategic alignment and drives business success.
- ❖ User Satisfaction - By addressing real user needs, AI systems enhance user satisfaction and adoption, leading to more effective solutions.
- ❖ Process Improvement - AI can streamline and optimise business processes, increasing efficiency and reducing operational costs.
- ❖ ROI - Focusing on value helps organisations achieve a higher return on investment (ROI) from their AI projects by ensuring resources are spent on impactful initiatives.
- ❖ Sustainability - Value-focused AI systems are more likely to be sustainable in the long term as they continuously adapt to meet evolving needs and deliver ongoing benefits.
- ❖ Stakeholder Confidence - Demonstrating tangible value builds confidence among stakeholders, fostering support for AI initiatives.

How to Apply

- ❖ Define Value Objectives - Clearly define what value means for the organisation and its stakeholders. This involves understanding business goals, user needs, and key performance indicators (KPIs) that will measure success.

❖ Adopt Value Driven Frameworks -Integrate wider value driven organisational level principles into the AI development process. Focus on co-creating value with customers and stakeholders.

❖ Identify Key Use Cases - Select AI use cases that have the highest potential for value creation. Prioritise projects based on their expected impact on business processes and user needs.

❖ Value Stream Mapping - Use value stream mapping to identify and eliminate waste in business processes. This helps in understanding where AI can add the most value by improving efficiency and effectiveness.

❖ User-Centric Design - Design AI systems with a focus on end-user needs and experiences. Engage users in the design and testing phases to ensure the AI system meets their expectations and requirements.

❖ Continuous Validation - Implement continuous validation mechanisms to assess the impact of AI systems. Use metrics and KPIs to measure performance, user satisfaction, and value delivery.

❖ Iterative Refinement - Based on validation results, iteratively refine and enhance AI systems. This ensures they remain aligned with business goals and continue to deliver value.

❖ Stakeholder Engagement - Maintain ongoing communication with stakeholders to understand their needs and expectations. Regularly report on AI initiatives' progress and impact, demonstrating their value contribution.

❖ Scalable Solutions - Develop scalable AI solutions that can grow with the organisation. Scalability ensures that as the

organisation evolves, the AI system can continue to deliver
value.

❖ Value-Focused Culture - Foster a culture that prioritises value
creation. Encourage teams to think about how their work
contributes to organisational goals and user satisfaction.

Focusing on value is essential for the success of AI initiatives. By
prioritising tangible value delivery, organisations can ensure their AI
systems address real user needs, improve business processes, and
drive strategic goals. Adopting ITIL 4 principles and emphasising
continuous evaluation and refinement helps align AI efforts with
organisational objectives, maximising their impact. A value-focused
approach not only enhances ROI but also builds stakeholder
confidence and supports sustainable, long-term AI success.

The 6 Guiding Principles

"Deep learning models are often described as 'black boxes,' making it difficult to understand how they arrive at specific decisions or outputs, which is a significant barrier to their broader adoption and reliability in critical applications." — *Gary Marcus*

The devil is in the detail, its time to sift him out!

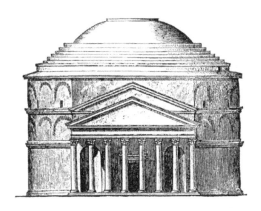

The 6 Pillars of Best Practice

The successful adoption and implementation of Generative AI hinge on a comprehensive approach that considers multiple, interrelated factors. The 6 Pillars of Best Practice for Generative AI—Sustainable and Cost-Effective, Secure and Ethical, Precise and Capable, Observe and Operate, Usability and User-Centricity, and Innovative and Resilient—serve as fundamental guidelines to navigate the complexities of AI deployment. While each pillar addresses a distinct aspect of AI system design and operation, they must be considered holistically to achieve optimal results.

These pillars are not isolated components but rather interconnected elements that work together to support the overall effectiveness of AI systems. For instance, robust security practices enhance the precision and reliability of AI models, while innovative approaches can drive usability improvements that lead to greater user engagement. Similarly, sustainable practices are crucial for enabling scalable AI solutions, and continuous monitoring ensures these systems remain resilient and cost-efficient over time.

By approaching these pillars as a cohesive framework, organisations can build AI systems that are technically sound, secure, user-friendly, scalable, and innovative. This integrated perspective ensures that AI technologies deliver consistent value, adapt to evolving needs, and operate within ethical and regulatory boundaries. Embracing the synergy between these pillars is essential for developing AI systems that are robust, trustworthy, and capable of driving meaningful outcomes in a rapidly advancing digital landscape.

Sustainable and Cost Effective

This pillar focuses on building sustainable and cost-effective AI systems throughout the adoption journey. It emphasises efficient resource use, optimal model selection, and environmentally conscious practices from the early planning stages to full-scale AI operations.

Secure and Ethical

This pillar ensures security, and ethical considerations are integrated at every stage of AI adoption. From the initial understanding of Generative AI to the final operationalisation, it guides organisations to implement robust security measures, maintain ethical standards, and comply with regulations.

Precise and Capable

This pillar ensures that AI systems are proven and capable at each step of adoption. It guides organisations to evaluate, test, and validate AI capabilities consistently, from initial experimentation to full integration into business processes.

Observe and Operate

This pillar emphasises the importance of observation and operational excellence across all stages of AI adoption. It provides frameworks for monitoring, logging, and maintaining AI systems from initial deployment to ongoing operations.

Usability and User-Centricity

This pillar ensures that AI systems remain contextual and user-centric throughout the adoption process. It guides organisations to consider user needs, context, and experience at every stage, from strategy formulation to full-scale implementation.

Innovative and Resilient

This pillar promotes innovation and resilience across all stages of AI adoption. It encourages experimentation, continuous learning, and adaptability, while also ensuring robustness and fault tolerance as AI systems scale and evolve.

Sustainable and Cost Effective

The Sustainable and Cost-Effective pillar focuses on building AI systems that are both economically viable and environmentally responsible. This pillar emphasises the importance of efficient resource utilisation, optimal model selection, and eco-friendly practices throughout the AI adoption journey, from initial planning to full-scale operations.

TOKEN MANAGEMENT

What is a Token?

In the context of Generative AI, a token is a unit of text that the model processes. Tokens can be as short as one character or as long as one word, depending on the language and context. They are the building blocks that AI models use to understand and generate text.

Why Is It Important?

Effective token management is crucial because it directly influences the cost and performance of AI operations. Excessive token usage can lead to increased large expenses and slower processing times.

Recommendations:

- ❖ Prompting – Use well-structured prompts (see the Precise and Capable Pillar for more on this) which focus on being specific as possible to reduce the amount of processing the LLM needs to conduct
- ❖ Predict – Model your expected production utilisation using a combination of load testing tools and tokeniser's which convert text to expect tokens.
- ❖ Monitoring Tools - Continuously monitor token consumption using tools and dashboards that track and analyse usage

patterns. Identify areas for improvement and adjust practices accordingly.

❖ Alerting – Set baselines and thresholds based on your expected workload

MODEL DEPLOYMENT

What is Model Deployment?

Model deployment involves the process of taking a trained AI model from development and making it operational in a production environment. This includes considerations for where and how the model is deployed to ensure it runs efficiently and sustainably.

Why Is It Important?

Sustainable model deployment is critical for ensuring that AI models operate at optimal efficiency with minimal environmental and financial costs. Proper deployment strategies help balance performance with resource utilisation, ultimately contributing to a lower carbon footprint and reduced operational costs.

Recommendations:

❖ Edge Deployment - Where feasible, deploy models on edge devices (e.g., smartphones, IoT devices) rather than relying solely on cloud-based services. Edge deployment reduces the need for constant data transfer and cloud processing, leading to lower latency, reduced bandwidth usage, and decreased energy consumption.

❖ Model Compression and Optimisation - Utilise model compression techniques such as pruning, quantisation, and knowledge distillation to reduce the size and complexity of models before deployment. Smaller, optimised models require less computational power and storage, making them more sustainable to run.

❖ Auto-Scaling and Resource Allocation - Implement auto-scaling and dynamic resource allocation strategies to verify that computing resources are only used when needed. This helps in avoiding the waste of idle resources and ensures that energy consumption is aligned with actual demand.

❖ Containerisation and Microservices - Deploy models using containerisation and microservices architectures. These approaches allow for more efficient use of computational resources, as they enable isolated deployment and scaling of model components based on demand.

❖ API-Driven LLMs - Consider using API-driven LLMs, which allow for scalable and flexible access to powerful models without the need to host or maintain the infrastructure yourself. This can lead to significant cost savings and lower environmental impact by leveraging the provider's optimised resources.

❖ Accuracy and Performance - Begin by testing the chosen LLM on your specific tasks and datasets to gauge its accuracy and effectiveness. Verify that the model meets your performance requirements without unnecessary overhead.

❖ Energy Consumption - Opt for LLMs that are optimised for energy efficiency to reduce the environmental footprint. Evaluate the energy consumption of the model during deployment and select options that align with your sustainability goals.

❖ Operational Cost - Conduct a thorough cost analysis that considers not only the subscription or usage fees of API-driven LLMs but also the long-term operational costs, including energy usage and infrastructure requirements. The goal is to balance cost-effectiveness with performance.

- ❖ Scalability and Flexibility - Choose an LLM that offers scalability and flexibility, allowing you to adjust resource allocation based on demand. This adaptability helps optimise costs over time and ensures that the model remains efficient as your needs evolve.
- ❖ Environmental Impact - Consider the environmental policies and practices of the LLM provider. Opt for LLMs developed by organisations committed to reducing carbon footprints, using renewable energy sources, or engaging in carbon offset initiatives.
- ❖ Monitoring and Feedback Loops - Continuously monitor the performance, resource usage, and energy consumption of deployed models. Establish feedback loops to regularly assess and optimise the model's deployment environment, adjusting as necessary to maintain efficiency.
- ❖ Disaster Recovery and Redundancy - Plan for disaster recovery and redundancy in a way that minimises resource duplication. Use strategies like geo-redundancy and efficient failover mechanisms that ensure availability while reducing unnecessary resource consumption.

By incorporating these strategies into your model deployment process, you can verify that your AI systems are not only effective and scalable but also sustainable and cost-efficient over the long term.

LIFECYCLE MANAGEMENT

What is Lifecycle Management?

Lifecycle management refers to overseeing the entire lifecycle of AI models, from development through deployment and maintenance, ensuring they remain efficient and effective.

Why Is It Important?

Proper lifecycle management ensures that AI models are updated, maintained, and eventually decommissioned in a cost-effective and sustainable manner. Failure to do so effectively could result in downtime.

Recommendations:

- ❖ Development to Deployment - Manage the entire lifecycle of AI models from development through deployment and maintenance. Verify that each phase is optimised for cost and sustainability.
- ❖ Version Control and Updates - Implement robust version control systems to manage model updates and ensure smooth transitions between different versions. Regularly update models to maintain performance and efficiency.
- ❖ End-of-Life Considerations - Plan for the end-of-life phase of AI models, including decommissioning and data archiving processes, to minimise waste and ensure responsible disposal of resources.

DATA EFFICIENCY

What is Data Efficiency?

Data efficiency in the context of Generative AI refers to the practice of optimising the amount, quality, and processing of data used to train and operate AI models. Efficient use of data not only reduces storage and computational costs but also minimises the environmental impact associated with data processing and storage.

Why Is It Important?

Effective data efficiency practices are crucial for controlling the costs and environmental footprint of AI operations. By ensuring that only necessary and high-quality data is used, you can avoid unnecessary processing, reduce storage needs, and enhance the performance of AI models.

Recommendations:

- ❖ Data Minimisation - Collect and process only the data necessary for training and operating your AI models. This reduces storage costs and processing times, leading to lower energy consumption and improved sustainability.
- ❖ Data Quality Assurance - Implement rigorous data quality checks to verify that the data used for training is accurate, relevant, and free from noise. High-quality data leads to better model performance, requiring fewer training cycles and thus reducing resource consumption.
- ❖ Synthetic Data Utilisation - Where possible, use synthetic data to augment your datasets. This reduces the need for extensive data collection from real-world sources, thereby lowering the environmental and ethical concerns associated with large-scale data harvesting.
- ❖ Federated Learning - Consider adopting federated learning approaches that enable model training on decentralised data sources. This approach minimises the need to centralise large datasets, reducing data transfer costs and preserving data privacy.

Data Archiving and Retention Policies: Implement clear policies for data archiving and retention, ensuring that only data necessary for current and future AI operations is retained. Regularly review and clean up outdated or unused data to free up storage and reduce ongoing costs.

By adhering to the principles and practices outlined in the Sustainable and Cost-Effective pillar, you can build AI systems that are not only financially viable but also environmentally responsible. This approach ensures that the benefits of Generative AI are realised without compromising on sustainability, paving the way for a more responsible and efficient future in AI technology.

Secure and Ethical

The Secure and Ethical pillar ensures that security and ethical considerations are integrated at every stage of AI adoption. From the initial understanding of Generative AI to the final operationalisation, this pillar guides you to implement robust security measures, maintain ethical standards, and comply with regulations.

JAILBREAKING

What is Jailbreaking?

In the context of Generative AI, jailbreaking refers to the act of manipulating an AI model to bypass its intended restrictions and controls, potentially leading to misuse or harmful outputs. This can compromise the ethical and functional boundaries set for the AI, resulting in unintended or malicious behaviour.

Why Is It Important?

Preventing jailbreaking is essential to verify that AI models operate within their intended ethical and functional boundaries, maintaining the integrity and trustworthiness of AI systems. Effective prevention of jailbreaking is vital to protect the AI from being exploited in ways that could cause harm or produce unethical outcomes.

Recommendations:

- ❖ Robust Controls
  - o Implement robust controls and safeguards to prevent jailbreaking attempts. This includes rigorous testing and validation processes to identify and mitigate

vulnerabilities.

- o Establish strict access controls and authentication mechanisms to restrict unauthorised access to the AI systems.

❖ Rigorous Testing

- o Regularly perform security assessments and penetration testing to identify potential weaknesses in the AI system. These tests should simulate various attack vectors to evaluate the system's resilience.
- o Use red teaming exercises where security experts attempt to jailbreak the AI to uncover vulnerabilities that might not be evident during regular testing.

❖ Validation Processes

- o Validate model behaviour under various scenarios to ensure it adheres to defined ethical and functional boundaries. This includes testing for edge cases and abnormal inputs that could trigger unintended behaviours.
- o Implement continuous validation techniques to monitor the AI's responses to new and evolving inputs, ensuring consistent adherence to ethical guidelines.

❖ Monitoring and Response

- o Continuously monitor AI model interactions for signs of jailbreaking attempts using advanced monitoring tools. Real-time monitoring is crucial to detect and respond to threats promptly.
- o Establish rapid response mechanisms to address any detected breaches, including automated alerts and predefined response protocols.

❖ Real-Time Monitoring

- o Use real-time monitoring tools to track model

outputs and user interactions. These tools should be capable of detecting unusual patterns that may indicate jailbreaking attempts.
- o Integrate anomaly detection systems that leverage machine learning to identify deviations from normal behaviour patterns.

❖ Incident Response Plan
- o Develop and implement a comprehensive incident response plan to quickly address and mitigate the impact of any jailbreaking attempts. This plan should outline the steps to be taken, roles and responsibilities, and communication protocols.
- o Conduct regular drills and simulations to ensure readiness and effectiveness of the incident response plan.

❖ Prompt Engineering
- o Implement prompt engineering techniques to create prompts that reduce the risk of producing harmful or inappropriate outputs. This involves using contextually aware and precise language.
- o Continuously refine prompt engineering practices based on feedback and observed model behaviour.

❖ User Training
- o Educate users on how to formulate queries that align with ethical and functional standards. Training should emphasise the importance of responsible AI usage and the potential consequences of misuse.
- o Provide resources and support to help users understand the best practices for interacting with the AI.

❖ Guardrails on Input and Output
- o Implement guardrails that operate on both the inputs

to and outputs from the LLM to ensure safety and compliance. Input validation and output filtering are critical components of these guardrails.

- o Validate and sanitise inputs to prevent harmful or inappropriate queries. This can involve using predefined filters and context-aware validation techniques.

TRAINING DATA IDENTIFICATION

What is Training Data Identification?

This involves understanding and documenting the sources and nature of the data used to train AI models, ensuring transparency and accountability.

Why Is It Important?

Knowing the origins and characteristics of training data is essential for assessing the quality, bias, and ethical implications of AI models. It also helps in complying with data protection regulations.

Recommendations:

- ❖ Data Documentation - Maintain comprehensive documentation of training data sources, including data provenance, quality, and any preprocessing steps. Ensure transparency in data handling practices.
- ❖ Source Tracking - Keep detailed records of where data was obtained and under what conditions it was collected.
- ❖ Metadata Management - Use metadata to document the characteristics and preprocessing steps applied to the data.
- ❖ Bias Assessment - Conduct regular assessments of training data to identify and mitigate biases. Implement strategies to

ensure diverse and representative datasets.
- ❖ Bias Detection Tools - Utilise tools designed to detect and quantify biases in training data.
- ❖ Diverse Data Collection - Verify that data collection processes include diverse and representative samples to minimise bias.

LOCATION AND DATA SOVEREIGNTY

What is Data Sovereignty?

Data sovereignty refers to the concept that data is subject to the laws and governance structures within the nation it is collected. This includes ensuring that data storage and processing comply with local regulations.

Why Is It Important?

Ensuring data sovereignty is critical for compliance with legal and regulatory requirements, protecting data privacy, and maintaining trust with users.

Recommendations:

- ❖ Regulatory Compliance - Adhere to local data sovereignty laws by ensuring data is stored and processed within the required jurisdictions. Implement geographical restrictions on data flows as necessary.
- ❖ Local Data Centres - Use data centres located within the required legal jurisdictions to store and process data.
- ❖ Geofencing - Implement geofencing techniques to control data flow based on geographical boundaries.
- ❖ Data Encryption -Use encryption techniques to secure data during transfer and storage, ensuring compliance with local regulations.

Secure and Ethical

COMPLIANCE

What is Compliance?

Compliance involves adhering to laws, regulations, and ethical guidelines that govern the use of AI and data. This includes industry-specific standards, data protection laws, and ethical guidelines.

Why Is It Important?

Maintaining compliance is crucial to avoid legal penalties, protect user privacy, and uphold ethical standards in AI operations.

Recommendations:

- ❖ Regulatory Awareness - Stay informed about relevant laws and regulations that impact AI operations. Regularly review and update compliance policies to reflect changes in the regulatory landscape.
- ❖ EU AI Act - Verify that AI systems comply with the EU AI Act, which outlines requirements for AI transparency, accountability, and fairness.
- ❖ GDPR - Adhere to the General Data Protection Regulation (GDPR) to protect user data privacy and security, including principles like data minimisation, purpose limitation, and user consent.
- ❖ ISO 42001 - Follow the guidelines of ISO 42001, an international standard for AI ethics and governance, to ensure responsible AI development and deployment.
- ❖ Acceptable Use Cases - Identify and document acceptable use cases for AI, ensuring that applications align with ethical standards and societal values.
- ❖ Training Programs - Conduct training programs to educate employees on ethical guidelines and compliance requirements.

- ❖ Audit and Review - Conduct regular audits and reviews to ensure compliance with regulatory and ethical standards. Use these audits to identify areas for improvement and to implement corrective actions.
- ❖ Internal Audits - Perform internal audits to assess compliance with established guidelines and standards.
- ❖ External Reviews- Engage third-party auditors to conduct independent reviews of AI practices and compliance measures.

PRIVACY BY DESIGN

What is Privacy by Design?

Privacy by Design is a proactive approach that ensures privacy is embedded into the design and architecture of AI systems from the outset. This principle integrates privacy protections directly into the AI development process to safeguard personal data throughout the AI application's lifecycle.

Why Is It Important?

Incorporating Privacy by Design is crucial for complying with data protection regulations such as GDPR and maintaining user trust. Embedding privacy into AI systems from the beginning helps mitigate risks related to data breaches, unauthorised access, and misuse of personal data.

Recommendations:

- ❖ Data Minimisation - Collect and process only the minimum amount of personal data necessary for the AI system's objectives, and implement automated data deletion processes to avoid unnecessary data retention.

- ❖ Anonymisation and Pseudonymisation - Use anonymisation

and pseudonymisation techniques to protect user identities and add an extra layer of privacy to the data handled by AI systems.

❖ User Consent Management - Obtain clear, explicit user consent before processing personal data, and provide easy-to-understand options for users to manage their data preferences.

❖ Privacy Impact Assessments (PIAs) - Regularly conduct Privacy Impact Assessments to evaluate privacy risks and ensure compliance with relevant data protection laws throughout the AI project.

❖ Access Controls - Implement strict access controls, using role-based access control (RBAC) to limit access to personal data based on job responsibilities, and regularly review access permissions.

SUPPLY CHAIN SECURITY

What is Supply Chain Security?

Supply Chain Security involves protecting AI systems from risks associated with third-party components, services, and data sources. This includes ensuring that all external elements integrated into the AI system meet stringent security and ethical standards.

Why Is It Important?

Supply Chain Security is vital for maintaining the integrity, security, and ethical standards of AI systems. The use of third-party components and data introduces potential vulnerabilities, making it essential to secure the supply chain to prevent data breaches, system compromises, and ethical violations.

Recommendations:

- ❖ Third-Party Vendor Assessment - Conduct thorough security assessments of all third-party vendors before integrating their products or services into your AI system. Evaluate their security practices and commitment to ethical standards.

- ❖ Contractual Safeguards - Include strict security and ethical requirements in contracts with third-party vendors, clearly outlining responsibilities for data protection, security practices, and incident response.

- ❖ Regular Audits and Monitoring - Implement ongoing monitoring and regular audits of third-party vendors and components to ensure continued compliance with security and ethical standards.

- ❖ Data Provenance and Integrity - Verify that all data sources used in AI models are trustworthy and free from tampering. Implement data provenance tracking and use checksums or cryptographic signatures to verify data integrity.

- ❖ Risk Management Strategy - Develop a comprehensive risk management strategy that addresses supply chain risks, including risk assessment, mitigation plans, and contingency measures for potential disruptions or security incidents.

By adhering to the practices outlined in the Secure and Ethical pillar, you can build AI systems that are not only secure but also ethically sound. This approach ensures that Generative AI technologies are developed and deployed responsibly, maintaining public trust and regulatory compliance while promoting ethical innovation.

Precise and Capable

The Precise and Capable pillar ensures that AI systems are thoroughly evaluated and validated at each step of adoption. This pillar guides you to consistently evaluate, test, and validate AI capabilities, from initial experimentation to full integration into business processes.

SEQUENCE ACCURACY PROBABILITY

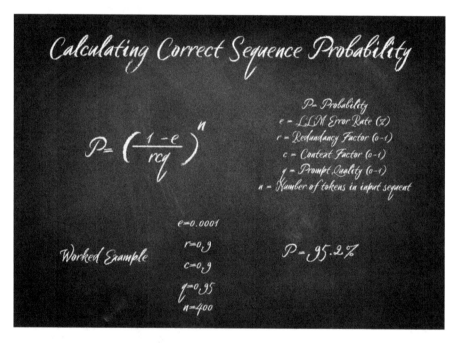

Calculating Correct Sequence Probability

$$P = \left(\frac{1-e}{rcq}\right)^{n}$$

P = Probability
e = LLM Error Rate (%)
r = Redundancy Factor (0–1)
c = Context Factor (0–1)
q = Prompt Quality (0–1)
n = Number of tokens in input sequent

Worked Example

$e = 0.0001$
$r = 0.9$
$c = 0.9$
$q = 0.95$
$n = 400$

$P = 95.2\%$

Figure 1 - Sequence Probability Equation

In the realm of Generative AI, achieving high-quality outputs from LLMs hinges on the model's ability to accurately predict the next word in a sequence. This process, often referred to as next-token prediction, is fundamental to generating coherent and contextually appropriate text. The challenge lies in ensuring that each predicted token (word) aligns correctly with the preceding context and contributes to the overall intended meaning.

Mechanisms Behind Sequence Accuracy Probability

At its core, the mechanism of an LLM involves predicting the next token in a sequence based on the given input context. This prediction is probabilistic, meaning the model assigns probabilities to a range of possible next tokens and selects the one with the highest probability. However, even with state-of-the-art models, there is an inherent error rate—sometimes the model will predict an incorrect token, which can lead to a cascade of errors in longer sequences.

To address this, we introduce the concept of Sequence Accuracy Probability. This novel approach quantifies the likelihood that a generated sequence of tokens will be entirely correct, given specific influencing factors. Sequence Accuracy Probability provides a more granular and comprehensive measure of an LLM's performance by considering not just the probability of individual token correctness but the cumulative effect over a sequence of tokens.

Key Influencing Factors

Several critical factors influence the Sequence Accuracy Probability:

❖ Baseline Error Rate (e): This is the inherent error rate of the LLM, indicating the probability that a single token is incorrect. It is determined by the model's architecture, training data, and the complexity of the task.

❖ Redundancy Factor (r): This measures the effectiveness of collaborative verification and error correction mechanisms. Higher redundancy implies better error mitigation, often achieved through techniques like ensemble methods or voting systems among multiple model outputs.

❖ Contextual Quality (**c**): This factor reflects how well the LLM leverages the provided context to reduce errors. High contextual quality indicates the model's proficiency in understanding and using context to inform its predictions, reducing the likelihood of contextually inappropriate tokens.

❖ Prompt Quality (**q**): The quality of the prompt provided to the model plays a significant role. High-quality prompts are clear, specific, and provide sufficient context, leading to better and more accurate responses from the LLM.

❖ Number of Tokens (**n**): The total number of tokens in the sequence being generated. Longer sequences inherently have more opportunities for errors to occur, so this factor is crucial in the overall probability calculation.

The Sequence Accuracy Probability Formula

To calculate the Sequence Accuracy Probability, we use the following formula:

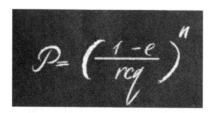

$$P = \left(\frac{1-e}{rcq} \right)^{n}$$

This formula integrates the baseline error rate, redundancy, contextual quality, prompt quality, and the length of the token sequence to provide a comprehensive measure of the likelihood that the entire sequence will be correct.

Let's consider a practical example:

Baseline Error Rate (e): 0.0001

Number of Tokens (n): 400

Contextual Quality Factor (c): 0.9

Redundancy Factor (r): 0.95

Prompt Quality Factor (q): 0.95

What you end up with is a probability of ≈ 0.952

Therefore, the probability that the entire sequence of 400 tokens is correct is approximately 95.2%.

Impact and Practical Implications

Understanding and improving Sequence Accuracy Probability has profound implications for the deployment and reliability of Generative AI systems. By focusing on key influencing factors like redundancy and contextual quality, you can significantly enhance the accuracy of language model outputs. This leads to more reliable and trustworthy responses, which is crucial for applications in fields such as legal, medical, and technical domains. Additionally, reducing errors through improved Sequence Accuracy Probability means less need for post-generation verification and correction, streamlining processes, and saving valuable time and resources.

By incorporating Sequence Accuracy Probability into the evaluation and refinement of AI systems, you can achieve higher standards of performance and reliability, ensuring that their AI-driven solutions meet the demands of real-world applications with greater confidence.

LLM SELECTION

Key Impact: Baseline Error rate (e)

What is LLM Selection?

LLM Selection in this context, involves choosing the most appropriate LLM for a specific task, with a focus on balancing performance, accuracy, and computational efficiency. The baseline error rate (e) of an LLM, which represents the inherent likelihood of generating incorrect tokens, is a critical factor in this selection process.

Why Is It Important?

Selecting the right LLM is vital because it directly influences the accuracy and reliability of AI outputs. A lower baseline error rate means fewer mistakes in token generation, leading to higher-quality results. This is particularly important in applications where precision is critical, such as legal, medical, or technical fields.

Recommendations:

❖ Evaluate Baseline Error Rate - To determine the baseline error rate of an LLM, perform benchmark testing using standard datasets and cross-validation techniques to calculate metrics like accuracy and precision. Additionally, conduct real-world testing with domain-specific data and pilot projects to understand the model's performance in practical scenarios.

❖ Task Alignment - Match the LLM's capabilities with the specific requirements of your task. Consider factors such as the model's training data, complexity, and ability to handle the context relevant to your domain.

❖ Performance vs. Resource Trade-off - Consider the

computational resources required by different LLMs. While more advanced models may offer lower error rates, they often demand higher computational power, which could impact efficiency.

MODULAR DEVELOPMENT

Key Impact: Redundancy Factor (r)

What is Modular Development?

Modular development, in the context of Generative AI, involves creating AI systems as a collection of independent, specialised agents, each designed to perform a specific task. This approach is akin to the microservices architecture in software development, where each agent operates autonomously yet interacts seamlessly with other agents to contribute to the overall system's functionality. The idea is to break down the AI system into smaller, manageable components that can be developed, deployed, and scaled independently, enhancing the system's overall flexibility and robustness.

Why is it Important?

Dividing an AI system into task-specific agents enhances flexibility, scalability, and resilience. This modular approach allows for the modification, upgrade, or replacement of individual components without disrupting the entire system, ensuring adaptability to changing requirements. Independent scaling of agents optimises resource use and supports seamless growth. The autonomy of each agent simplifies troubleshooting and maintenance, reducing downtime and accelerating issue resolution. Additionally, the system's resilience is improved, as the failure of one agent doesn't impact the entire system, while parallel development of agents accelerates the overall development process.

Recommendations:

- ❖ Identify Tasks - Begin by breaking down the overall functionality of your AI system into discrete, manageable tasks that can be handled by individual agents. This involves thoroughly analysing the AI's objectives and the processes required to achieve them. Each task should be distinct and capable of being independently executed by an agent.
- ❖ Design Agents - Define the scope, responsibilities, and interfaces of each agent. Verify that each agent has a clear, focused role and that it can operate autonomously while interacting seamlessly with other agents. Design agents to be specialised in specific functions, such as data processing, natural language understanding, or image generation.
- ❖ Develop Modular Components - Implement each agent as a separate, modular component, following the principles of microservices architecture. Verify that each agent is loosely coupled, meaning it can be developed, deployed, and scaled independently of the others. This modular approach allows for more agile development and easier updates.
- ❖ Ensure Interoperability - Establish robust communication protocols and APIs to facilitate seamless interaction between agents. This is essential to verify that all agents work together harmoniously to achieve the system's overall goals. Proper interoperability ensures that the system functions cohesively, even as individual agents are updated or replaced.
- ❖ Iterate and Optimise - Continuously monitor the performance of individual agents and the system as a whole. Make iterative improvements to enhance functionality, efficiency, and integration. Regular performance evaluations and optimisations help verify that the system remains

scalable, maintainable, and aligned with evolving business needs.

❖ Leverage Collaboration - Encourage teams to work concurrently on different agents, leveraging the modular nature of the system. This not only speeds up development but also fosters a collaborative environment where teams can focus on their specialised areas while contributing to the overall success of the project.

Adopting an agentic-based approach in Generative AI development fosters a modular, scalable, and maintainable architecture. By breaking down AI systems into specialised agents, organisations can enhance flexibility, improve resilience, and accelerate innovation. This principle not only streamlines development processes but also ensures that AI solutions are robust, adaptable, and aligned with evolving business needs.

PROMPT ENGINEERING

Key Impact: Prompt Quality Factor (q) and Number Of Tokens (n)

What is Prompt Engineering?

Prompt engineering involves the meticulous design and crafting of input prompts to guide AI models in generating desired responses. Effective prompt engineering ensures that AI outputs are accurate, relevant, and aligned with user intentions, ultimately enhancing the performance and reliability of AI systems.

Why Is It Important?

Prompt engineering is vital because it directly impacts the quality and dependability of AI outputs. Well-crafted prompts significantly improve AI model performance, reduce misunderstandings, and enhance user satisfaction by providing clear guidance on the desired response.

Recommendations:

- ❖ Utilise the COSTRE Framework - The COSTRE framework provides a structured approach to creating effective prompts. It stands for Context, Objective, Style, Tone, Audience, and Response. Here's how to apply each component:
- ❖ Context (C):
  - o Provide the AI with background information to ensure it understands the situation or scenario. This includes relevant details and any prior information necessary for generating a coherent response.
  - o Example: "In the context of customer support for a tech product..."
- ❖ Objective (O):
  - o Clearly define the task to direct the AI's focus. Specify the main goal you want the AI to achieve.
  - o Example: "Provide a detailed troubleshooting guide for resolving connectivity issues..."
- ❖ Style (S):
  - o Specify the desired writing style to align the AI's response with the intended presentation or format.
  - o Example: "Use a step-by-step instructional style..."
- ❖ Tone (T):
  - o Set the tone to ensure the response resonates with the required sentiment or emotion.
  - o Example: "Use a friendly and professional tone..."
- ❖ Response (R):
  - o Provide the response format, such as text or JSON, to ensure the AI outputs the response in the desired

structure, facilitating integration into pipelines or other systems.
  - o Example: "Format the response as JSON..."
- ❖ Example (E):
  - o Provide an exact example of what you would like the AI to produce for you. This is a key step and really helps the attention mechanisms within the LLM.
- ❖ Craft Clear and Concise Prompts
  - o Simplicity - Use straightforward language to avoid ambiguity. Complex or vague prompts can lead to misunderstandings and poor-quality outputs.
  - o Specificity - Be precise about what you want the AI to do. Include necessary details and avoid generalisations that could result in irrelevant or inaccurate responses.
  - o Iterative Testing and Refinement
- ❖ Initial Testing - Test initial prompts with the AI model to see how it responds. Analyse the outputs to identify areas for improvement.
- ❖ Refinement - Adjust prompts based on test results. Modify wording, structure, and content to enhance the quality of AI responses.
- ❖ Continuous Improvement - Continuously test and refine prompts as new use cases and requirements emerge. Keep track of what works best for different scenarios.
- ❖ Examples - Provide examples within prompts to guide the AI. Examples help the model understand the desired format and content of the output.
- ❖ Templates - Develop reusable templates for common tasks. Templates ensure consistency and efficiency in prompt creation.
- ❖ Leveraging Advanced Techniques

Precise and Capable

- o Dynamic Prompts - Use dynamic prompts that adjust based on context and user inputs. This can enhance the relevance and accuracy of AI responses.
- o Multi-Turn Dialogues - For complex tasks, design prompts to handle multi-turn dialogues, where the AI maintains context across multiple interactions.

By mastering prompt engineering and applying the COSTRE framework, you can significantly enhance the performance and reliability of your Generative AI systems. This practice ensures that AI outputs are aligned with user expectations and business objectives, fostering greater trust and satisfaction in AI-driven solutions.

FINE-TUNING

Key Impact: Contextual Quality Factor (c)

What is Fine-Tuning?

Fine-tuning is the process of adapting a pre-trained AI model to a specific task or domain by training it further on a smaller, task-specific dataset.

Why Is It Important?

Fine-tuning enhances the model's performance on specific tasks, making it more relevant and accurate for the intended application.

Recommendations:

- ❖ Data Preparation - Collect and preprocess a high-quality, task-specific dataset for fine-tuning.
- ❖ Training Process - Use transfer learning techniques to further train the pre-trained model on the new dataset, adjusting hyperparameters as needed.
- ❖ Evaluation and Iteration - Evaluate the fine-tuned model's

performance and iterate as necessary to achieve the desired accuracy and relevance.

CONTEXT WINDOWS

Key Impact: Contextual Quality Factor (c)

What are Context Windows?

Context windows refer to the portion of input text that an AI model can consider at once to generate a response. Larger context windows allow the model to understand and generate more coherent and contextually relevant outputs.

Why Is It Important?

Using appropriate context windows ensures that the AI model captures sufficient context, leading to more accurate and relevant responses.

Recommendations:

❖ Determining Window Size - Analyse the nature of tasks and typical input lengths to determine the optimal context window size.

❖ Sliding Windows - Implement sliding window techniques for longer texts, where the model processes overlapping segments to maintain context to work around recall challenges.

❖ Contextual Management - Use techniques to manage and preserve context across multiple interactions or sessions. Remember as a rule of thumb the more tokens utilised in a single interaction the lower the Sequence Accuracy Probability will be.

Precise and Capable

RETRIEVAL-AUGMENTED GENERATION (RAG)

Key Impact: Contextual Quality Factor (c)

What is Retrieval-Augmented Generation (RAG)?

RAG is a hybrid approach that enhances generative AI models by incorporating relevant external information retrieved from databases, search engines, or other data sources. This method allows the AI to generate responses that are not only based on its training data but also enriched with real-time or specific contextual information.

Why Is It Important?

RAG significantly improves the accuracy, relevance, and contextuality of AI-generated responses, making it particularly valuable for applications requiring precise and up-to-date information. It helps overcome the limitations of purely generative models, which may not always have the latest information or specific details needed for certain queries.

Recommendations:

* ❖ Document Retrieval
    * ○ Data Sources - Identify and integrate relevant data sources that can provide the necessary context for the AI model. These sources could include internal databases, external knowledge bases, APIs, and web search engines.
    * ○ Retrieval Mechanisms - Develop and implement efficient retrieval mechanisms using search algorithms, retrieval models, or pre-trained retrievers like BM25 or dense retrieval models.
    * ○ Query Processing - Design query processing systems

to effectively interpret and transform user queries into formats suitable for retrieval systems.

- ❖ Integration with Generative Models
  - ○ Contextual Embedding - Embed retrieved documents or data into the input context for the generative model. This can involve concatenating retrieved texts with the original query or using more sophisticated integration methods.
  - ○ Model Fine-Tuning - Fine-tune generative models to effectively utilise the embedded context, ensuring they can incorporate and generate responses based on the additional information.
  - ○ Hybrid Generation - Implement hybrid generation techniques where the model generates initial responses and then refines them using the retrieved context to improve accuracy and relevance.

- ❖ Evaluation and Optimisation
  - ○ Performance Metrics - Establish metrics to evaluate the performance of the RAG system, such as precision, recall, relevance, and response time.
  - ○ Continuous Monitoring - Continuously monitor the system's performance, using these metrics to identify areas for improvement.
  - ○ Iterative Refinement - Regularly update and optimise both the retrieval and generative components based on evaluation results, user feedback, and changes in data sources.

- ❖ Anomaly Detection and Correction
  - ○ Consistency Checks - Implement mechanisms to check for inconsistencies or anomalies in the generated outputs, especially when incorporating retrieved information.

Precise and Capable

- o Correction Mechanisms - Develop automated or semi-automated correction mechanisms to address detected anomalies and ensure the reliability of responses.
- ❖ User Feedback Integration
  - o Feedback Collection - Collect user feedback on the quality and relevance of AI-generated responses.
  - o Adaptive Learning - Use feedback to adapt and improve the retrieval and generation processes, ensuring the system evolves with user needs and preferences.

PERFORMANT OUTPUT

What is Performant Output?

Performant output refers to the ability of AI systems to generate high-quality results efficiently, considering factors like hosting infrastructure, data volume, and data quality.

Why Is It Important?

Ensuring performant output is critical for delivering timely and reliable AI services that meet user expectations and business requirements. The performance of AI models affects not only the quality of the generated outputs but also the overall efficiency and cost-effectiveness of the system.

Recommendations:

- ❖ Optimised Hosting Solutions - Choose hosting solutions that provide the necessary computational power and scalability without over-provisioning. Options include cloud-based hosting, on-premises infrastructure, and hybrid solutions. Optimised hosting ensures that resources are used efficiently, reducing costs and environmental impact.

❖ Data Management and Processing Pipelines - Manage data volume effectively to verify that AI models can process and generate outputs efficiently. This includes optimising data storage, processing pipelines, and handling real-time data streams. Efficient data management reduces latency and improves the speed of AI responses.

❖ High-Quality Data Inputs - Ensure high data quality by implementing robust data cleaning, preprocessing, and validation techniques. High-quality input data leads to more accurate and reliable AI outputs, reducing the need for extensive post-processing.

❖ LLM Selection Based on Performance - Select the most suitable LLM based on a balance between performance metrics (such as accuracy and speed) and computational efficiency. This ensures that the model chosen is capable of delivering high-quality outputs without unnecessary resource expenditure.

❖ Prompt Optimisation - Develop precise and well-crafted prompts to guide the AI models. Precise prompts reduce ambiguity, improve the relevance and accuracy of the generated outputs, and optimise the number of tokens processed, contributing to both accuracy and efficiency.

Useable and User-Centric

The Useable and User-Centric pillar ensures that AI systems remain focused on user needs and context throughout the adoption process. This pillar guides you to consider user requirements, contextual relevance, and overall user experience at every stage, from strategy formulation to full-scale implementation.

EVALUATION DRIVEN DEVELOPMENT

Figure 2 - Evaluation Driven Development

What is Evaluation Driven Development?

Evaluation Driven Development (EDD) involves defining metrics and criteria to measure the performance and effectiveness of AI systems before building and deploying them. This structured approach ensures that AI systems are developed with clear performance goals in mind, leading to reliable, high-quality outputs that align with business objectives.

Why Is It Important?

By establishing clear evaluation criteria from the outset, you can verify that their AI systems are aligned with business objectives, perform reliably, and deliver value. This proactive approach helps in identifying potential issues early in the development process, ensuring that the final AI system meets the required standards and expectations. Moreover, EDD promotes a culture of continuous improvement, where performance metrics guide ongoing refinements and enhancements.

Recommendations:

- ❖ Define Metrics
    - o Establish Specific Metrics - Identify and define specific metrics to evaluate AI performance. Common metrics include accuracy, precision, recall, response time, and scalability.
    - o Align with Business Goals - Verify that the chosen metrics align with business goals and user expectations. This alignment helps in prioritising performance aspects that are most critical to organisational success.
    - o Context-Specific Metrics - Consider context-specific metrics that reflect the unique requirements of the task or application. For example, in a customer service AI, user satisfaction scores and resolution times might be relevant.
- ❖ Build Systems to Meet Metrics
    - o Design with Metrics in Mind - Develop AI systems with the predefined metrics as core design principles. This involves integrating performance goals into the design, implementation, and testing phases.
    - o Performance-Oriented Development - Focus development efforts on achieving the defined performance standards. Use metrics as benchmarks to guide decisions during system architecture, model

selection, and feature engineering.

- o Iterative Testing - Continuously test the system against the metrics throughout the development process. Early and frequent testing helps in identifying deviations from expected performance, allowing for timely corrections.

❖ Routine Evaluation

- o Implement Continuous Monitoring - Establish processes for continuous evaluation of AI performance against the established metrics. This involves deploying monitoring tools that provide real-time insights into system performance.
- o Feedback Loops - Create feedback loops where evaluation results inform iterative improvements. Regularly assess the AI system's performance and make necessary adjustments to optimise outcomes.
- o Periodic Audits - Conduct periodic performance audits to verify that the AI system remains aligned with the defined metrics and business goals. These audits help in identifying long-term trends and potential areas for improvement.

❖ Adaptive Refinement

- o Iterative Refinement - Use the results from continuous evaluation to guide iterative refinements. This involves updating models, tuning parameters, and improving data quality based on performance feedback.
- o Scalability Considerations - As the system evolves, verify that it can scale effectively to handle increased workloads without compromising on the established performance metrics.
- o User Feedback Integration - Incorporate user

feedback into the evaluation process to understand real-world performance and user satisfaction. This feedback is crucial for refining the AI system to better meet user needs.

❖ Tool Integration
- ○ Automated Evaluation Tools - Utilise automated tools to streamline the evaluation process. These tools can provide real-time metrics tracking, anomaly detection, and performance visualisation.
- ○ Integrated Development Environments (IDEs) - Leverage IDEs that support evaluation-driven development, offering built-in functionalities for defining, tracking, and analysing performance metrics.

❖ Stakeholder Communication
- ○ Transparent Reporting - Regularly communicate performance metrics and evaluation results to stakeholders. Transparency helps in building trust and ensuring that all parties are aware of the AI system's capabilities and limitations.
- ○ Collaborative Reviews - Involve stakeholders in performance reviews and decision-making processes. Collaborative efforts can lead to more informed and balanced improvements.

❖ Relay The Benefits
- ○ Alignment with Business Goals - Ensures that AI systems are developed with clear objectives that support organisational success.
- ○ Enhanced Reliability - Promotes the creation of robust and dependable AI systems that perform consistently under varying conditions.
- ○ Proactive Issue Identification - Helps in identifying and addressing potential issues early in the

development process, reducing the risk of costly post-deployment fixes.
- o Continuous Improvement - Encourages an ongoing cycle of assessment and refinement, leading to progressively better AI systems.
- o User Satisfaction - Aligning metrics with user expectations leads to higher user satisfaction and better adoption rates.

GENAI TESTING

What is GenAI Testing?

GenAI testing involves systematically testing generative AI models to ensure they produce accurate, reliable, and safe outputs. This includes both pre-deployment and ongoing testing.

Why Is It Important?

Rigorous testing is essential to identify and address potential issues, such as biases, inaccuracies, and unintended behaviours, before they impact users or business processes.

Recommendations:

- ❖ Pre-Deployment Testing - Conduct comprehensive tests on AI models before deployment. This includes functional testing, performance testing, security testing, and user acceptance testing.
- ❖ Ongoing Testing - Implement mechanisms for ongoing testing of AI models in production to monitor performance and detect any emerging issues. This includes regular audits and retraining processes.
- ❖ Scenario-Based Testing - Use scenario-based testing to

evaluate how AI models perform under various conditions and edge cases. This helps in identifying and mitigating potential risks and weaknesses.

❖ User Feedback - Collect feedback from users on the quality of AI outputs. Use this feedback to further refine and improve prompts.

❖ Automated Feedback - Implement automated feedback mechanisms to monitor AI performance and identify areas for prompt enhancement.

PERSONALISATION

What is Personalisation?

Personalisation involves tailoring AI-generated content and interactions to individual users based on their preferences, behaviour, and history.

Why Is It Important?

Personalisation enhances user engagement, satisfaction, and the overall user experience by providing relevant and customised interactions.

Recommendations:

❖ User Profiling - Collect and analyse user data to create detailed profiles, including preferences, behaviour patterns, and historical interactions.

❖ Personalised Content Generation - Use AI models to generate content and responses tailored to individual user profiles.

❖ Feedback Loops - Implement feedback mechanisms to continuously refine and improve personalisation based on user responses and behaviour.

USER EXPERIENCE DESIGN

What is User Experience (UX) Design?

UX design focuses on creating AI systems and interfaces that are intuitive, user-friendly, and provide a positive user experience.

Why Is It Important?

Good UX design is essential for ensuring that AI systems are accessible, easy to use, and meet user expectations.

Recommendations:

❖ User Research - Conduct thorough user research to understand the needs, preferences, and pain points of target users.
❖ Prototyping and Testing - Develop prototypes of AI interfaces and conduct usability testing to gather feedback and make iterative improvements.
❖ Design Principles - Apply UX design principles such as simplicity, consistency, and accessibility to create intuitive interfaces.

USER CHANNELS

What are User Channels?

User channels refer to the various platforms and mediums through which users interact with AI systems, such as web applications, mobile apps, chatbots, and voice assistants.

Why Is It Important?

Supporting multiple user channels ensures that AI systems are accessible to a broader audience and can meet users where they are.

Recommendations:

- ❖ Multi-Channel Strategy - Develop a strategy for supporting multiple user channels, considering the specific requirements and best practices for each channel.
- ❖ Consistent Experience - Ensure a consistent and seamless user experience across all channels, maintaining coherence in interactions and responses.
- ❖ Channel Optimisation - Optimise AI systems for each user channel, leveraging the strengths and addressing the limitations of each platform.

Observe and Operate

The Observe and Operate pillar emphasises the importance of observation and operational excellence across all stages of AI adoption. This pillar provides frameworks for monitoring, logging, and maintaining AI systems from initial deployment to ongoing operations, ensuring that these systems deliver consistent value and reliability.

TRANSPARENCY

What is Transparency?

Transparency in AI systems refer to the clarity and openness regarding how AI models make decisions and generate outputs. It involves documenting model behaviours, data sources, and decision-making processes.

Why Is It Important?

Transparency is crucial for building trust with users, ensuring accountability, and facilitating regulatory compliance.

Recommendations:

- ❖ Documentation - Maintain detailed documentation of AI models, including their training data, algorithms, and decision-making processes.
- ❖ Explainability Tools - Use tools and techniques to provide explanations of AI model outputs, helping users understand how decisions are made.
- ❖ Open Communication - Foster open communication with stakeholders about AI system capabilities, limitations, and performance metrics.

CONTINUOUS EVALUATION

What is Continuous Evaluation?

Continuous evaluation involves regularly assessing AI systems to spot changes in quality, detect anomalies, and ensure consistent performance.

Recommendations:

Continuous evaluation helps maintain the reliability and accuracy of AI outputs, linking closely with other pillars to ensure overall system quality.

How?

- ❖ Regular Assessments - Conduct regular assessments and audits of AI systems to evaluate performance and detect deviations.
- ❖ Automated Evaluation Tools - Utilise automated tools and techniques to continuously monitor AI outputs and performance metrics.
- ❖ Anomaly Detection - Implement GenAI-based anomaly detection systems to identify and address unusual patterns or behaviours.

REALTIME AI SECURITY MONITORING

What is Realtime AI Security Monitoring?

Real-time monitoring involves continuously tracking AI systems and their interactions to promptly detect any signs of jailbreaking attempts. It ensures that AI models are operating within their intended restrictions and ethical boundaries by providing immediate insights into their behaviour.

Why Is It Important?

Real-time monitoring is essential for protecting AI systems from security threats and misuse. By detecting suspicious activities as they happen, it allows for immediate response and mitigation, preventing potential harm and maintaining the integrity and trustworthiness of the AI system.

Recommendations:

- ❖ Deployment of Monitoring Tools
    - o Utilise advanced monitoring tools capable of real-time data analysis. These tools should be integrated into the AI system to continuously track interactions and outputs.
    - o Ensure these tools can handle high volumes of data and provide timely analysis without significant latency.
- ❖ Anomaly Detection Systems
    - o Implement AI-based anomaly detection systems to identify deviations from normal behaviour patterns. These systems can learn from historical data to recognise unusual activities that might indicate jailbreaking attempts.
    - o Use adaptive algorithms that continuously improve their detection capabilities as more data becomes available.
- ❖ Automated Alert Systems
    - o Configure automated alert systems to notify security teams immediately upon detecting potential jailbreaking attempts. Alerts should be sent through

multiple channels, such as email, SMS, and dashboards, to ensure prompt attention.
- o Set up customisable alert thresholds to balance sensitivity and specificity, minimising false positives while ensuring genuine threats are flagged.

❖ Log Analysis and Correlation
- o Implement comprehensive logging of all interactions with the AI model, including inputs, outputs, and user actions. Logs should provide a detailed audit trail to help trace the origin and nature of any security incidents.
- o Use log analysis tools to correlate data from different sources and identify patterns that might indicate an ongoing or attempted jailbreak.

❖ Incident Response Integration
- o Integrate real-time monitoring with an incident response system to enable swift action. The incident response plan should outline steps to be taken when an alert is triggered, including containment, investigation, and remediation procedures.
- o Regularly review and update the incident response plan based on feedback and insights gained from real-time monitoring data.

❖ Dashboard and Visualisation
- o Create a centralised dashboard that provides a real-time overview of AI system activity. Visualisation tools can help security teams quickly understand the status and identify any anomalies at a glance.
- o Ensure the dashboard is customisable to focus on the most critical metrics and alerts specific to potential jailbreaking activities.

❖ Feedback Loops

Observe and Operate

- o Establish feedback loops where insights from real-time monitoring and alerts are used to refine and improve monitoring tools and algorithms. Continuous learning from detected incidents can enhance the system's ability to identify and respond to future threats.

INTEROPERABILITY

What is Interoperability?

Interoperability refers to the ability of AI systems to work seamlessly with other systems, applications, and data sources.

Why Is It Important?

Ensuring interoperability enhances the flexibility and scalability of AI systems, enabling integration with existing workflows and technologies.

Recommendations:

- ❖ Standardised Protocols - Use standardised communication protocols and data formats to facilitate integration with other systems.
- ❖ APIs - Develop robust APIs (Application Programming Interfaces) to enable seamless data exchange and interoperability.
- ❖ Modular Architecture - Design AI systems with modular architecture to allow easy integration and compatibility with various technologies.

MANAGING AGENTS

What is Managing Agents?

Managing agents involves overseeing the deployment and operation of numerous AI agents within an organisation, ensuring coordinated management and monitoring.

Why Is It Important?

As organisations spin up many AI agents, it becomes essential to manage them effectively to avoid chaos and verify consistent performance.

Recommendations:

- ❖ Single Pane of Glass - Implement a unified management interface to provide a comprehensive view of all AI agents, facilitating easier monitoring and control.
- ❖ Centralised Management - Use centralised tools and platforms to manage the lifecycle, performance, and security of AI agents across the organisation.
- ❖ GenAIOps Integration - Verify that managing agents is a key part of GenAIOps, integrating seamlessly with other pillars for a holistic approach to AI operations.

CI/CD FOR GENAI

What is CI/CD for GenAI?

Continuous Integration and Continuous Deployment (CI/CD) for Generative AI involves automating the testing, integration, and deployment of AI models to guarantee rapid and reliable updates.

Why Is It Important?

Implementing CI/CD practices in GenAI is essential for maintaining the agility and quality of AI systems, enabling rapid iteration and minimising downtime.

Recommendations:

- ❖ Automated Testing - Develop automated testing pipelines to validate AI models during integration, ensuring they meet performance and safety standards.
- ❖ Continuous Integration - Implement continuous integration practices to merge code changes frequently, reducing integration issues and improving collaboration.
- ❖ Continuous Deployment - Automate the deployment process to make certain that updates are rolled out smoothly and efficiently, minimising disruptions and enabling quick feedback cycles.

HARNESSING EVALUATION DRIVEN DEVELOPMENT IN CI/CD FOR GENAI

Evaluation Driven Development (EDD) from the Usability and User-Centricity Pillar can be harnessed within the CI/CD pipeline to ensure AI models meet predefined standards and goals. By defining clear metrics and criteria to measure performance and effectiveness before deployment, you can verify AI systems align with business objectives and deliver value. Establishing specific metrics such as accuracy, precision, recall, response time, and scalability, and developing AI systems to meet these metrics, allows for continuous evaluation and improvement. Integrating EDD into the CI/CD pipeline enables regular assessment of AI performance against established metrics, guiding iterative improvements and refinements, thus maintaining high standards and reliability.

By adhering to the principles and practices outlined in the Observe and Operate pillar, you can verify their AI systems are transparent, well-monitored, secure, interoperable, and effectively managed. This approach promotes operational excellence and reliability, ensuring that AI technologies deliver consistent value and remain trustworthy throughout their lifecycle.

Innovative and Resilient

The Innovative and Resilient pillar promotes innovation and resilience across all stages of AI adoption. This pillar encourages experimentation, continuous learning, and adaptability, while ensuring robustness and fault tolerance as AI systems scale and evolve.

FOSTERING A CULTURE OF GENAI EXPERIMENTATION

What is a Culture of Experimentation?

A culture of experimentation involves creating an environment where continuous exploration, testing, and innovation are encouraged and supported.

Why Is It Important?

Encouraging experimentation leads to innovative solutions, improved AI capabilities, and the discovery of new applications and use cases.

Recommendations:

* ❖ Encourage Creativity - Promote a mindset that values creative thinking and exploration among teams. Implement brainstorming sessions, hackathons, and innovation contests to stimulate creative thinking and idea generation.
* ❖ Provide Resources - Allocate resources such as time, funding, and tools to support experimental projects and initiatives. Provide access to cutting-edge tools and technologies that support experimentation, such as advanced AI platforms, data analytics tools, and computing resources.
* ❖ Safe-to-Fail Environment - Create an environment where failure is seen as a learning opportunity, reducing the fear of experimentation. Foster an environment where failure is seen

124

as a natural part of the innovation process and an opportunity to learn and improve. Affirm that leadership supports and encourages experimentation, providing guidance and resources while allowing teams the freedom to explore.

CONTINUOUS GENAI LEARNING AND IMPROVEMENT

What is Continuous Learning and Improvement?

Continuous learning involves regularly updating AI systems with new data, insights, and techniques to improve their performance and adaptability.

Why Is It Important?

Continuous improvement ensures that AI systems remain relevant, effective, and competitive in a rapidly changing technological landscape.

Recommendations:

❖ Regular Updates - Implement processes for regularly updating AI models with new data and retraining them to maintain accuracy and relevance. Continuously integrate new data into the AI model training process to keep models up-to-date and regularly retrain models with the latest data.

❖ Feedback Loops - Establish feedback loops to gather insights from users and system performance, using this information to inform improvements. Collect feedback from users to understand their experiences and identify areas for improvement. Implement monitoring tools to track AI system performance and identify trends and patterns that can inform updates and improvements.

❖ Stay Informed - Keep abreast of the latest advancements in

Innovative and Resilient

AI research and technology, integrating new techniques and methodologies as they become available. Invest in R&D to explore new AI techniques and methodologies. Promote knowledge sharing within the organisation through workshops, seminars, and internal publications.

SCALABILITY AND DISASTER RECOVERY

What is Scalability and Disaster Recovery?

Scalability ensures that AI systems can handle increasing workloads and expand seamlessly, while disaster recovery involves preparing for and mitigating the impact of failures or disasters.

Why Is It Important?

Ensuring scalability and disaster recovery is crucial for maintaining uninterrupted and reliable AI services, particularly as systems grow and evolve.

Recommendations:

❖ Scalable Infrastructure - Design AI systems with scalable infrastructure that can grow with demand. Use cloud services and distributed computing to manage workload increases efficiently. Utilise cloud services that offer scalability, allowing you to increase or decrease resources based on demand. Implement distributed computing solutions to manage workload distribution and enhance system performance.
❖ Redundancy and Backup - Implement redundancy and backup systems to establish data and service continuity in case of failures. Safeguard data redundancy by storing copies of data in multiple locations to prevent data loss. Implement

system redundancy to verify that critical components have backups that can take over in case of failure.

* ❖ Disaster Recovery Planning - Develop comprehensive disaster recovery plans, including regular drills and simulations to validate preparedness for potential disruptions. Conduct regular disaster recovery drills to test the effectiveness of your plans and verify preparedness.
* ❖ Multiple LLM Selection for Redundancy - Integrate multiple LLMs endpoints from different regions to enhance system resilience. By having alternative models ready, you can switch between them in case of performance issues or failures.
* ❖ Cloud-Native Practices - Adopt cloud-native practices such as containerisation and microservices architecture to enhance flexibility and scalability. Using Kubernetes for container orchestration can help manage workloads efficiently and validate that applications are resilient to infrastructure changes and failures.
* ❖ Version Control - Use version control systems like Git to manage changes to the codebase, enabling collaboration and ensuring that changes can be tracked and rolled back if necessary.
* ❖ Continuous Integration and Continuous Deployment (CI/CD) - Implement CI/CD pipelines to automate the testing, integration, and deployment of AI models. This ensures that updates can be delivered quickly and reliably, with minimal disruption.
* ❖ Automated Testing - Develop comprehensive automated test suites to validate AI models and code changes. This includes unit tests, integration tests, and end-to-end tests to verify that all components function correctly and integrate seamlessly.
* ❖ Code Reviews - Conduct regular code reviews to verify that

best practices are followed and to identify potential issues early. Peer reviews help improve code quality and foster knowledge sharing among team members.

❖ Documentation - Maintain clear and up-to-date documentation for all aspects of the AI system, including architecture, code, and operational procedures. Good documentation facilitates easier maintenance, onboarding of new team members, and knowledge transfer.

❖ Security Best Practices - Incorporate security best practices into every stage of the SDLC. This includes conducting regular security audits, using secure coding practices, and implementing access controls to protect sensitive data.

❖ Agile Methodologies - Adopt agile methodologies to enable iterative development and continuous feedback. Agile practices such as sprint planning, daily stand-ups, and retrospectives help teams stay aligned and responsive to changing requirements.

By adhering to the principles and practices outlined in the Innovative and Resilient pillar, organisations can foster a culture of experimentation, establish continuous learning and improvement, and maintain scalable and resilient AI systems. This approach promotes innovation, adaptability, and robustness, enabling AI technologies to thrive and evolve in a dynamic environment.

The 6 Pillars of Best Practice

"AI is one of the most important things humanity is working on. It is more profound than electricity or fire" — Sundar Pichai

It may seem like we are in the future with this AI revolution, but it's just begun – let's look forward to a future where we can tell our ironing to do itself!

Future Perspectives in GenAIOps

Exploring GenAIOps provides a comprehensive foundation for developing and operationalising generative AI systems, but the journey of GenAIOps is far from static. As AI technology continues to evolve rapidly, it's crucial to look ahead and consider the future trends and advancements that will shape this field. This final section explores potential directions for GenAIOps, emphasising continuous learning, ethical considerations, and the integration of emerging technologies.

Evolving AI Capabilities

The capabilities of generative AI models are expected to grow exponentially. Future models will likely possess even greater accuracy, contextual understanding, and creativity, opening up new applications and possibilities. Keeping abreast of these advancements and integrating them into the GenAIOps framework will be essential.

Enhanced Contextual Understanding

Future AI models will better understand and retain context over longer interactions, improving the relevance and coherence of generated content. This advancement will facilitate more natural and meaningful conversations, leading to superior user experiences.

Multimodal AI Systems

The integration of text, image, audio, and video generation capabilities within a single AI system will offer more holistic solutions. For instance, a single AI could generate a marketing campaign that includes written content, visual graphics, and audio jingles, all aligned with the same creative vision.

Real-time Adaptation

AI systems will increasingly be able to adapt in real-time to changing inputs and environments, providing more dynamic and responsive interactions. This capability will be particularly beneficial in environments that require immediate feedback and adjustments, such as customer service or interactive learning platforms.

Ethical and Responsible AI

As generative AI becomes more powerful, the importance of ethical and responsible AI practices will only increase. Ensuring fairness, transparency, and accountability in AI systems will remain a top priority.

Bias Mitigation

Developing advanced techniques to detect and reduce biases in AI models, ensuring fair and equitable outcomes. This will involve not only technical solutions but also ongoing audits and evaluations to monitor AI behaviour and impact.

Transparent Decision-Making

Enhancing the transparency of AI systems to make their decision-making processes more understandable to users. This includes developing tools that can explain how and why an AI reached a particular conclusion or generated a specific output.

Regulatory Compliance

Staying updated with evolving regulations and standards to validate ongoing compliance and ethical integrity. As global standards evolve, it will be crucial for organisations to adapt their AI systems to meet these new requirements, ensuring they operate within legal and ethical boundaries.

Integration with Emerging Technologies

The future of GenAIOps will be shaped by the integration of generative AI with other emerging technologies, creating synergistic effects that amplify the impact of AI solutions.

Synergistic Technologies

❖ Blockchain - Leveraging blockchain for secure, transparent, and tamper-proof data management in AI systems. Blockchain can validate the integrity of data used for training and decision-making, enhancing trust and reliability.

❖ Internet of Things (IoT) - Integrating generative AI with IoT devices to provide smarter, more contextually aware solutions in various domains such as smart homes, healthcare, and industrial automation. AI can analyse data from IoT devices to provide real-time insights and actions.

❖ Quantum Computing - Exploring the potential of quantum computing to solve complex problems faster and more efficiently, enhancing the performance of generative AI models. Quantum computing could significantly reduce the time required for training large AI models, enabling more rapid innovation.

Continuous Learning and Adaptation

The pace of AI development necessitates a commitment to continuous learning and adaptation. Organisations must foster a culture that embraces ongoing education, experimentation, and iteration.

Strategies for Continuous Improvement:

- ❖ Lifelong Learning - Encouraging AI models to continuously learn from new data and experiences to remain relevant and effective. Implementing systems that allow AI to update its knowledge base regularly will ensure it stays current with the latest information and trends.
- ❖ Iterative Development - Implementing agile methodologies to facilitate rapid prototyping, testing, and refinement of AI systems. This approach allows for quick adjustments based on feedback and changing requirements.
- ❖ Collaborative Ecosystems - Building collaborative ecosystems that include researchers, developers, and end-users to drive innovation and address real-world challenges effectively. Collaboration can lead to the sharing of best practices and the development of more robust and versatile AI solutions.

Preparing for the Future

Preparing for the future of GenAIOps involves not only anticipating technological trends but also fostering resilience and flexibility within organisations. This includes investing in infrastructure, training, and change management to adapt to new advancements smoothly.

Preparation Steps

* ❖ Infrastructure Readiness - Ensuring that the technological infrastructure is scalable and adaptable to support future AI developments. This involves leveraging cloud services and scalable architectures that can grow with the organisation's needs.
* ❖ Workforce Training - Providing continuous education and training programs to equip the workforce with the necessary skills to work with advanced AI technologies. Training should cover not only technical skills but also ethical considerations and best practices in AI deployment.
* ❖ Change Management - Developing robust change management strategies to navigate the organisational shifts required by new AI capabilities and processes. Effective change management can help mitigate resistance and establish smooth transitions.

Conclusion and Outlook

The future of GenAIOps is bright and full of potential. By staying informed about emerging trends, committing to ethical practices, integrating new technologies, and fostering a culture of continuous learning, organisations can harness the full power of generative AI. This proactive approach will verify that AI initiatives remain innovative, impactful, and aligned with both business goals and societal values.

As we look ahead, the insights and methodologies presented in this book will continue to evolve. A further exploration will delve deeper into these future trends, providing updated frameworks, advanced techniques, and new case studies to guide organisations in the next phase of their generative AI journey. Stay tuned for further advancements and expanded content that will help you navigate the ever-evolving landscape of generative AI with confidence and expertise.

By preparing for these future developments, organisations can not only keep pace with technological advancements but also lead the way in innovative and responsible AI practices. The journey of GenAIOps is ongoing, and with each iteration, we move closer to realising the full potential of generative AI in transforming industries and enhancing human capabilities.

ABOUT THE AUTHOR

Written in third person, like a pro!

About The Author

Harrison is the CTO and co-founder of Great Wave AI and the visionary author behind the Exploring GenAIOps. With over 14 years in the tech industry, Harrison has established himself as a leader in the development and implementation of cutting-edge Generative AI technologies. He also leads The Centre for GenAIOps CIC, a community-driven initiative dedicated to advancing Generative AI through active engagement and feedback.

As a DevOps Ambassador, Harrison has been deeply involved in the DevOps movement, which has greatly influenced his approach to GenAIOps. His expertise spans application development, database management, and managing complex cloud and on-premise infrastructures. Harrison's leadership has driven the successful delivery of strategic projects, from conceptualisation to deployment, ensuring alignment with business goals and adherence to the highest standards of security and scalability.

Harrison's journey in technology is marked by a focus on innovation, leveraging the latest tools to set new industry standards. His strategic vision not only encompasses the adoption of advanced technologies but also integrates these advancements into transformative business practices. Throughout his career, Harrison has built and led high-performance teams, fostering cultures of innovation that are essential for growth in the dynamic tech sector.

In Exploring GenAIOps, Harrison combines his deep technical expertise with his DevOps background to create a comprehensive guide for integrating AI into operational strategies. His work reflects a commitment to aligning technology initiatives with broader business objectives, driving significant outcomes, and contributing to overall business growth.

About The Author

Contact: Harrison.kirby@outlook.com

Note: This book will continue to be updated. If you would like the latest copy Free of Charge please email using the above address.

ABOUT THE AUTHOR

www.ingramcontent.com/pod-product-compliance
Lightning Source LLC
LaVergne TN
LVHW051245050326
832903LV00028B/2580